W9-CHR-374

BANGKOK
ENCOUNTER

AUSTIN BUSH

Bangkok Encounter

Published by Lonely Planet Publications Pty Ltd
ABN 36 005 607 983

Australia	Locked Bag 1, Footscray,
(Head Office)	Vic 3011
	☎ 03 8379 8000 fax 03 8379 8111
USA	150 Linden St, Oakland, CA 94607
	☎ 510 250 6400
	toll free 800 275 8555
	fax 510 893 8572
UK	2nd fl, 186 City Rd
	London EC1V 2NT
	☎ 020 7106 2100 fax 020 7106 2101
Contact	talk2us@lonelyplanet.com
	lonelyplanet.com/contact

This 3rd edition was written by Austin Bush. Austin also
wrote the 2nd edition. China Williams authored the 1st
edition. This book was commissioned in Lonely Planet's
Melbourne office and produced by: **Commissioning
Editor** Ilaria Walker **Coordinating Editor** Carolyn
Boicos **Coordinating Cartographer** Csanad Csutoros
Layout Designer Yvonne Bischofberger **Assisting
Editor** Janet Austin **Managing Editor** Annelies
Mertens **Managing Cartographer** Amanda Sierp
Senior Editor Susan Paterson **Cover Research** Sabrina
Dalbesio **Internal Image Research** Rebecca Skinner
Managing Layout Designer Jane Hart **Thanks to**
Bruce Evans, Lisa Knights, Shawn Low

Cover photograph Th Yaowarat, Chinatown, Austin
Bush/Lonely Planet Images

All images are copyright of the photographers unless
otherwise indicated. Many of the images in this guide
are available for licensing from Lonely Planet Images:
lonelyplanetimages.com

10 9 8 7 6 5 4 3 2 1   3rd edition
ISBN: 978 1 74179 821 0   Printed in China

MIX
Paper from
responsible sources
FSC™ C021741
www.fsc.org

Paper in this book is certified against the Forest Stewardship
Council™ standards. FSC™ promotes environmentally
responsible, socially beneficial and economically viable
management of the world's forests.

HOW TO USE THIS BOOK
Colour-Coding & Maps

Colour-coding is used for symbols on maps
and in the text that they relate to (eg all eating venues on the maps and in the text are
given a green knife and fork symbol). Each
neighbourhood also gets its own colour, and
this is used down the edge of the page and
throughout that neighbourhood section.

Shaded yellow areas on the maps denote areas of interest – for their historical
significance, their attractive architecture or
their great bars and restaurants. We encour-
age you to head to these areas and just start
exploring!

Prices

Multiple prices listed with reviews (eg
100/50B) indicate adult/child.

Send us your feedback We love to hear from travellers –
your comments keep us on our toes and help make our
books better. Our well-travelled team reads every word on
what you loved or loathed about this book. Although we
cannot reply individually to postal submissions, we always
guarantee that your feedback goes straight to the appropriate authors, in time for the next edition. Each person who
sends us information is thanked in the next edition, and
the most useful submissions are rewarded with a free book.

Visit **lonelyplanet.com** to submit your updates and sug-
gestions or to ask for help. Our award-winning website also
features inspirational travel stories, news and discussions.

Note: We may edit, reproduce and incorporate your comments in Lonely Planet products such as guidebooks,
websites and digital products, so let us know if you don't
want your comments reproduced or your name acknowl-
edged. For a copy of our privacy policy visit lonelyplanet.
com/privacy.

AUSTIN BUSH

Austin came to Thailand in 1998 on a language scholarship to Chiang Mai University. The lure of city life, employment and spicy food eventually led Austin to Bangkok. City life, employment and spicy food have managed to keep him there since. Austin is a native of Oregon and a freelance writer and photographer who often focuses on food; samples of his work can be seen at www.austinbushphotography.com.

AUSTIN'S THANKS

Thanks to the folks at Lonely Planet, including Ilaria Walker, David Connolly and Bruce Evans, to the previous author of this book, China Williams, not to mention to the kind people on the ground in Bangkok, including Prempreeda Pramoj Na Ayutthaya, Richard Hermes, Wesley Hsu, Natchaphat Itthi-chaiwarakom, Gene Kasidit, Nym Punlopruksa, Maher Satter, David Thompson, Pailin Wedel, Patrick Winn and Sirin P Wongpanit.

Our readers Many thanks to the travellers who wrote to us with helpful hints, useful advice and interesting anecdotes. Brendan Dempsey, Kristine Gapay, Rochelle Hogan, Trent Paton, Fred Prager, Michelle White.

A meditative stroll through the streets of bustling Ko Ratanakosin (p40)

CONTENTS

THIS IS BANGKOK

Bangkok is excess in all of its unrestrained glory. Bigger, better, more: the city is insatiable, a monster that feeds on concrete, shopping malls and diesel exhaust.

The city demands that you be in the present and in the moment, not necessarily for a religious epiphany, but because the city is self-absorbed and superficial, blissfully free of wrinkle-inducing self-reflection. Smiles and sà·nùk (the Thai word for 'fun') are the key passports into Bangkok society. A compliment here, a joke there – the demands of social lubrication in this megalopolis are more akin to a small village than an anonymous city, and are a necessity for survival.

As Bangkok forcefully kneads out of you all demands for order and predictability, you'll understand the famous Thai smile. It is the metaphorical brakes on the urban overdrive. Packed into these concrete corridors are religious spectacle, unapologetic consumerism and multi-flavoured hedonism – corrupting and purifying souls within footsteps of each other. A tragicomic confluence of human desires and aspirations best viewed through a detached smile.

Of the famous and infamous attractions, Bangkok's best feature is its intermingling of opposites. A modern world of affluence orbits around a serene traditional core. Step outside the four-star hotels into a typical Siamese village where taxi drivers knock back energy drinks and upcountry transplants grill chicken on a streetside barbecue. Hop a BTS train to the glitzy shopping malls where trust-fund babies examine luxury brands as carefully as the housewives inspect produce at the open-air markets. Or appreciate the attempts at enlightenment at the city's famous temples and doorstep shrines, or simple acts of kindness amid the urban bustle.

You can jump between all of these worlds – wining and hobnobbing at a chic club, eating at a streetside market, getting plucked and pummelled into something more beautiful, or sweating profusely on a long unplanned march. Bangkok is an urban connoisseur's dream come true.

Top left Take your pick at Pak Khlong Market (p74) **Top right** Funky protection ware: amulets for all Thais **Bottom** Fearsome demons guard the gilded chedi (stupa) at Wat Phra Kaew (p42)

MICHAEL COYNE / LONELY PLANET IMAGES ©
The majestic Grand Palace (p10) is the former royal residence

>1 GRAND PALACE & WAT PHRA KAEW

MAKE A PILGRIMAGE TO THAILAND'S PRINCELY BUDDHA

Wat Phra Kaew (p42) is an elaborate and colourful temple that easily distracts first-time visitors from the namesake figure: the Emerald Buddha, a diminutive statue carved of nephrite (a type of jade, not emerald) housed in the main hall. This is one of the most revered of the Thai Buddhas, representing the legitimacy of the reigning dynasty and claiming a swashbuckler's history. The dazzling figure was discovered in northern Thailand in the 15th century when a stupa was split open by lightning. To conceal its lustre the figure was covered in plaster (a common practice during the days of wars and bandits). Succeeding generations eventually forgot what the plaster hid inside until an accidental fall revealed the contents. In the mid-16th century, Laotian invaders stole the sacred Buddha but the Thais retrieved it in battle and used it to bestow divine approval on General Taksin, who assumed the throne after the fall of Ayuthaya. The figure was placed in its present location during the reign of Rama I (King Buddha Yodfa; r 1782–1809), the first king in the Chakri dynasty, when the capital was moved across the river from Thonburi to Bangkok in 1782.

Because of its royal status, the Emerald Buddha is ceremoniously draped in monastic robes, which are changed every season (hot, wet and cool) by the king or the crown prince.

AN EPIC CHALLENGE: THE RAMAKIAN

In the corners of Wat Phra Kaew are murals of the *Ramakian* story, the Thai version of the Indian epic *Ramayana*. The tale unfolds clockwise from the northern gate and each frame depicts the main event in the centre with the conclusion depicted either above or below.

The story begins with the hero, Rama (the green-faced character), and his bride Sita (the beautiful topless maiden). The young couple are banished to the forest, along with Rama's brother. In this pastoral setting, the evil king Ravana (the character with many arms and faces) disguises himself as a hermit in order to kidnap Sita.

Rama joins forces with Hanuman, the monkey king (logically depicted as the white monkey), to attack Ravana and rescue Sita. Although Rama has the pedigree, Hanuman is the unsung hero. He is loyal, fierce and clever. En route to the final fairy-tale ending, great battles and schemes of trickery ensue until Ravana is finally killed. After withstanding a loyalty test of fire, Sita and Rama are triumphantly reunited.

GREG ELMS / LONELY PLANET IMAGES ©

Next door to Wat Phra Kaew is the Grand Palace (p42), a vast compound where successive kings, their families and attendants lived until Rama V (King Chulalongkorn; r 1868–1910) moved the royal seat to what is now known as Dusit Palace Park (p22). The primary buildings display a fusion of Thai and Western architectural styles and are occasionally used for official functions, but the formal grounds lack the vibrancy of the neighbouring temple.

A strict dress code is enforced at the temple; see the boxed text on p44 for guidelines and more information.

>2 MAE NAM CHAO PHRAYA

TRAVEL WITH THE COMMONERS ALONG THE RIVER OF KINGS

Central Thais are river people, building their homes, livelihoods and capitals along the waterways. One such artery is the Mae Nam Chao Phraya (literally the 'River of Kings'), which starts in the mountains of northern Thailand, sweeps past the former capital of Ayuthaya and defines the western boundary of Bangkok before it reaches the Gulf of Thailand some 370km away from its source.

The river is always teeming with activity: hulking freighter boats trail behind dedicated tugs, elegant longtail boats skip across the wake, and children practise cannonballs into the muddy water. The residents claiming a waterfront view range from world-class hotels to sweaty warehouses and auspicious temples. As evening sets in, cool river breezes mellow the harsh temperatures and the blinding sun slips into serene streaks of reds and golds. From this vantage point, sooty Bangkok suddenly looks beautiful.

The best way to explore the watery side of Bangkok is aboard the river express boat (p184), which sprints from as far south as Wat Ratchasingkhon to Nonthaburi in the north. At docks along the way, the ferry discharges crowds of map-toting tourists, commuting

LONGTAIL SAFARI

For an up-close view of the city's famed canals, longtail boats are available for hire at Tha Chang, Tha Tien, Tha Oriental and Tha Phra Athit. Prices at Tha Chang are the highest and allow little room for negotiation, but you stand the least chance of being taken for a ride or being hit up for various tips and other fees.

Trips explore the Thonburi canals of Khlong Bangkok Noi and Khlong Bangkok Yai, taking in the Royal Barges National Museum (p43), Wat Arun (p44) and a riverside temple with fish feeding. Longer trips diverge into Khlong Mon, between Bangkok Noi and Bangkok Yai, which offers more typical canal scenery, including orchid farms. Some trips stop at a snake farm, and on weekends you will have the option of visiting a floating market.

However, it's worth pointing out that to actually disembark and explore any of these sights, the most common one-hour tour (1000B, up to six people) is simply not enough time and you'll most likely need 1½ (1300B) or two hours (1600B). Most operators have set tour routes, but if you have a specific destination in mind, you can request it.

TOM COCKREM / LONELY PLANET IMAGES ©

office clerks and groups of monks. (The back of the starboardside is reserved for monks; women should opt for the portside.)

Start an upriver journey from Tha Sathon, accessible via the BTS Saphan Taksin station. On your right is the old *fa·ràng* (Westerner) quarter – referred to as Riverside in this book – first inhabited by seafarers and multinational shipping companies. The Oriental Hotel and other neoclassical buildings are a few of the remaining memorials to this era, when the water was the main thoroughfare.

Around Tha Ratchawong, the river brushes up against Chinatown (p16) and its cubby-holed warehouses where goods are unloaded the old-fashioned way – by hand.

After a while, striking Wat Arun (p44) looms on your left and then ornate Grand Palace and Wat Phra Kaew (p10) on your right – forming a triangular convergence of sacred sites.

North of Saphan Phra Ram VIII, an elegant suspension bridge, the concrete dissipates into greenery and sunburned temples. The final stop is Nonthaburi, the launching point for boat trips to sleepy Ko Kret (p138).

>3 WAT PHO

JOSS STICKS AND MASSAGE: BANGKOK'S TEMPLE OF TRADITIONAL MEDICINE

Wat Phra Kaew gets all the spotlight, but Wat Pho (p44) is everyone's favourite. Rarely crowded, the rambling grounds of Wat Pho claim a 16th-century birthday, predating the city itself. It is also the country's biggest temple. Still not impressed? How about Wat Pho's primary Buddha – a reclining figure that nearly dwarfs its sizeable shelter. Symbolic of Buddha's death and passage into nirvana, the reclining Buddha, 46m long and 15m high, is gilded with gold leaf. Lining the soles of the feet is a magnificent mother-of-pearl inlay depicting the 108 auspicious *lák·sà·nà* (traits) that signify the birth of a predestined Buddha.

The Buddha images on display in the other four *wí·hǎhn* (sanctuaries) are worth a nod. Particularly beautiful are the Phra Chinnarat and Phra Chinnachai Buddhas, both from Sukhothai, in the west and south *bòht* (chapels). The galleries extending between the four chapels feature no fewer than 394 gilded Buddha images, many of which display Ayuthaya or Sukhothai features. The remains of Rama

TAKE A LOAD OFF

During the reign of Rama III (King Nang Klao; r 1824–51), Wat Pho was dedicated as an open university and continues to serve as the national headquarters for the teaching and preservation of traditional Thai medicine and massage. Nearby stone inscriptions showing yoga and massage techniques still remain in the temple grounds, serving their original purpose as visual aids. Fittingly, the temple is also home to two massage pavilions, where visitors queue for the privilege of being twisted and pounded into submission. If this scholarly environment has inspired you, a few blocks away from the temple is the Wat Pho Thai Traditional Medical & Massage School (p46), where the curious can learn these ancient skills via several multiday courses.

I are interred in the base of the presiding Buddha image located in the *bòht*.

The granite giants in the courtyard of Wat Pho are perhaps Thailand's oldest immigrants. These statues arrived aboard Chinese ships as ballast in the hulls and were left behind on the return trip. Some are warriors, others philosophers and one is said to be Marco Polo.

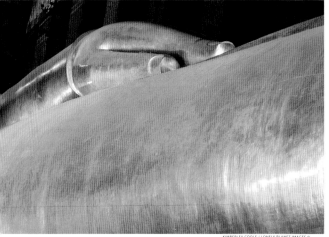

KIMBERLEY COOLE / LONELY PLANET IMAGES ©

>4 CHINATOWN

PERFECT THE ART OF GETTING LOST WITH THE EMPEROR OF COMMERCE

Chinatown (p70) is pure energy bundled into blazing neon signs, belching buses and full-on commerce. Each block specialises in a certain product: rubber bath plugs here, guns and ammo there, and painted signs and coffins on another block. Not much is souvenir-worthy but all of this small-scale industry in one place is rarer these days than bound feet.

The main artery, Th Yaowarat, lends its name to the district and is crowded with gold shops – sealed glass-front buildings looking more

---

THE CHINESE INFLUENCE

In many ways Bangkok is as much a Chinese city as it is Thai. The presence of the Chinese in Bangkok dates back to before the founding of the city, when Thonburi Si Mahasamut was little more than a Chinese trading outpost on the Chao Phraya River. In the 1780s, during the construction of the new capital under Rama I (King Buddha Yodfa; r 1782–1809), Hokkien, Teochew and Hakka Chinese were hired as coolies and labourers. The Chinese already living in the area were relocated to the districts of Yaowarat and Sampeng, today known as Bangkok's Chinatown.

During the reign of Rama I, many Chinese began to move up in status and wealth. They controlled many of Bangkok's shops and businesses and, because of increased trading ties with China, were responsible for an immense expansion in Thailand's market economy. Visiting Europeans during the 1820s were astonished by the number of Chinese trading ships in the Chao Phraya River, and some assumed that the Chinese formed the majority of Bangkok's population.

The newfound wealth of certain Chinese trading families created one of Thailand's first elite classes that was not directly related to royalty. Known as *jôw sŏo-a*, these 'merchant lords' eventually obtained additional status by accepting official posts and royal titles, as well as offering their daughters to the royal family. Today it is thought that more than half of the people in Bangkok can claim some Chinese ancestry.

During the reign of Rama III (King Nang Klao; r 1824–51), the Thai capital began to absorb many elements of Chinese food, design, fashion and literature. The growing ubiquity of Chinese culture, coupled with the tendency of the Chinese men to marry Thai women and assimilate into Thai culture, meant that by the beginning of the 20th century there was relatively little that distinguished many Chinese from their Siamese counterparts.

GREG ELMS / LONELY PLANET IMAGES ©

like Chinese altars than downtown jewellers. Wat Mangkon Kamalawat (p73) venerates both Chinese and Thai deities. Another revered temple is Wat Traimit (p74), famous for its golden Buddha.

There's more life behind the cacophonous arteries. Sampeng Lane (p75) is now a wholesale market, but it used to be a red-light district.

Trok Itsaranuphap (Talat Mai; p72) is the shortest, greatest stroll in the city; the alley begins near Talat Kao (Old Market), which claims mythic longevity, and eventually leads to stalls selling ritual offerings for the deceased. Tucked behind River City shopping centre, the area known as Talat Noi (between Th Songwat and Th Si Phraya; p96) is a labyrinth of machine-repair shops and pencil-thin footpaths.

>5 WAT MAHATHAT & AMULET MARKET

BANGKOK'S COMMUNAL MEDICINE CUPBOARD FOR THE SPIRIT, MIND AND BODY

Most tourists skip the area north of Wat Phra Kaew, eager to tick off more famous attractions elsewhere, but nowhere in this conflicted city is the daily practice of Thai Buddhism more alive than in the crowded corridors around Wat Mahathat (p44). All aspects of the religion – from the sacred study of scripture and daily meditation to the folk beliefs in lucky charms – are modestly on display for the cultural wanderer.

Rambling Wat Mahathat is the most important centre of Buddhist learning in Southeast Asia because of the Buddhist university on the site, Mahathat Rajavidyalaya, which educates monks from Laos, Cambodia and Vietnam and is the national centre of the Mahanikai monastic sect (one of the two sects that make up the Sangha, or Buddhist brotherhood, in Thailand).

Wat Mahathat was built in the Ayuthaya period, but very little of it appears historically striking; its attraction is its role in the community, with daily comings and goings of laity and monks. Lots of foreigners wander onto the grounds looking for the daily meditation courses (p46) and the resident English-speaking monks make enthusiastic guides.

Outside the temple gates on Th Maha Rat is a daily Amulet Market (dà·làht prá krêuang; p47) selling wearable protection from evil spirits or bad fortune. It has the ambience of a flea market but the collections are as highly prized as rare antiques. Most of the amulets are medallions embossed with images of Buddha, Hindu deities or famous monks, and carry with them protective powers to stop bullets, ensure fertility or reap material success. Thais working in high-risk professions, such as cab drivers and

---

TAKING THE CURE

Along Th Maharat are closet-sized shops that sell traditional Thai medicines, typically made of herbs and employing the philosophies of Ayurvedic and Chinese healing traditions. Commercial formulas sold at these shops contain ingredients you're more likely to meet in a Thai curry: galangal and lemon grass, which can treat everything from bad breath to stomach ulcers.

---

construction workers, are some of the most reliable amulet buyers, as these images are more trusted than Western-style insurance policies. But it's rare to meet a Bangkok Thai who doesn't wear some type of amulet.

Being so close to Thammasat University, the market also caters to student needs as well. Alongside a bin of Buddha amulets are stores selling graduation caps and gowns and further back along the river are squatty student-cheap restaurants that sneak a peek of the river.

HIGHLIGHTS

AUSTIN BUSH / LONELY PLANET IMAGES ©

>6 FOOD MARKETS, RESTAURANTS & STREET STALLS

DINE ALFRESCO IN THE BIG MANGO

Bangkok's reputation as one of the most polluted cities in the world belies its forte as an outdoor dining capital. Despite the modern conveniences of air-conditioning and fashion cafes, some of the most memorable meals in the city that's also called the Big Mango are had at the tried-and-true markets and food stalls that make it possible to nibble the day away. Forget about three square meals; when in Bangkok, locals snack throughout the day, packing away at least four meals before sunset.

Like a sundial, the sidewalk landscape of food stalls is an approximate indication of the time of day. In the mornings, vendors sell steaming cups of thick filtered coffee sweetened with condensed milk, or mini baton-shaped doughnuts dunked in glasses of warm soy milk. By midday the buffet has switched to premade rice and curries, made-to-order rice dishes and fruit snacks. Once the traffic and the heat subside (relatively speaking), the dining social hour begins, with sleepy lanes being converted into communal dinner

---

BEYOND THE STREET STALL

Read any food magazine article about eating in Thailand, and you will inevitably find gushing references to the glories of the country's street food. While much of the food sold from mobile carts and streetside stalls is indeed very tasty, it certainly isn't the case that *only* street food is good. In fact, in our research, we've found that the best places to eat are anything but mobile, but rather are the long-standing, family-owned restaurants typically found in aged Sino-Portuguese shophouses.

The cooks at places such as Nay Mong (p76) or Roti-Mataba (p60) have likely been serving the same dish, or limited repertoire of dishes, for several decades, and really know what they're doing. The food may cost slightly more than you'll pay on the street, but the setting is usually more comfortable and hygienic, not to mention the fact that you're eating a piece of history. While such restaurants rarely have English-language menus, you can usually point to a picture or dish. If that fails, you'll get the chance to practise your Thai.

So do indulge in a street cart or two, they're a fun part of the Thailand experience, but be sure to try a few old-school restaurants as well.

GREG ELMS / LONELY PLANET IMAGES ©

tables. Friends gather around plastic tables and slurp down shared dishes or bowls of noodles chased with bottles of beer or fruit juices. Perhaps no other dining experience will leave such a lasting impression as an alfresco meal complete with a spice-induced sweat moustache.

Vendor carts can be found in every nook and cranny of the city. Popular food markets include Or Tor Kor (p139), Soi 38 Night Market (p128) and Chinatown (see the boxed text, p75).

>7 DUSIT PALACE PARK

ESCAPE HYPERACTIVE BANGKOK AMID A PALACE OF VICTORIAN GEMS

No other spot in Bangkok is as pretty and peaceful as Dusit Palace Park (p67), a three-dimensional scrapbook made by Rama V of his European tour. Ushering in a new millennium, Rama V moved the royal residence from the ancient confines of the Grand Palace to this Europe-inspired complex, which is now open to the public and filled with museums honouring the former king and Thai cultural traditions. Beyond its historical attributes, Dusit Palace is a much-needed respite from Bangkok's teeming energy.

The most famous palace building is the enormous golden-teak mansion, Vimanmek Palace (p68), which was used by the king and his wife, children and concubines as their primary home. Vimanmek Palace's 81 rooms are elegant and overwhelmingly pastel. But the highlight, besides the architecture, is seeing Rama V's personal effects and antiques – among them grand pianos, Ching-dynasty pieces and the first menu in Thailand – and getting an insight into how the royals lived.

Reflecting the king's ingenious use of Western influences, Abhisek Dusit Throne Hall (p66) is a tasteful melange of Moorish and Victorian

---

ARCHITECTURAL ETHICS

Thailand has made numerous admirable efforts to preserve historic religious architecture, from venerable old stupas to ancient temple compounds. The Department of Fine Arts in fact enforces various legislation that makes it a crime to destroy or modify such monuments, and even structures found on private lands are protected.

On the other hand, Thailand has less to be proud of in terms of preserving secular civil architecture such as old government offices and shophouses. Only a few of Bangkok's Ratanakosin and Asian Deco buildings have been preserved, along with a handful of private mansions and shophouses, but typically only because the owners of these buildings took the initiative to do so. Thailand has little legislation in place to protect historic buildings or neighbourhoods, and distinctive early Bangkok architecture is disappearing fast, often to be replaced by plain cement, steel and glass structures of little historic or artistic value. For an illustrated list of buildings in Thailand that have received government protection, seek out the coffee-table book *174 Architectural Heritage in Thailand* (Saowalak Phongsatha Posayanan/Siam Architect Society, 2004).

GREG ELMS / LONELY PLANET IMAGES ©

styles with a distinctly Thai character. Today the hall is used to exhibit a collection of regional handicrafts.

Near the Th Ratchawithi entrance, two residence halls display the HM King Bhumibol Photography Exhibitions, collections of photographs and paintings by the present monarch. Among many loving photos of his wife and children are also historic pictures of the king playing the clarinet with Benny Goodman and Louis Armstrong in 1960. Further along is the Ancient Cloth Museum (p66) and tucked away beside the Th U Thong Nai exit is the Royal Thai Elephant Museum (p67).

The domed neoclassical building at the foot of Royal Plaza is Ananta Samakhom Throne Hall (p66), built in the early 1900s by Italian architects in the style of European government houses. Used today to display handicrafts, the throne hall also hosted the first meeting of the Thai parliament until its meeting place was moved to a facility nearby.

Because Dusit Park is royal property, visitors must dress appropriately (long pants or skirts, and shirts with sleeves); sarongs are available if your lower half isn't covered enough.

>8 CHATUCHAK WEEKEND MARKET

SHOP AT THE BEHEMOTH OF ASIAN-STYLE MARKETS

A rambling flea market of bargains, Chatuchak Weekend Market (p138) is Bangkok's biggest and most intense market. Imagine supersizing the average Thai market with its narrow passageways lined with merchandise, and you've got a close approximation of Chatuchak. Silks, extra-small fashions, fighting cocks and fighting fish, fluffy puppies and souvenirs for the insatiable *fa·ràng* – if it can be sold in Thailand, you'll find it here. From everyday to clubby, clothes dominate most of the market, where young designers unveil their wares. Look out for secondhand clothes that have obviously emigrated from Western closets.

Your wallet may already be chomping at the bit, but go prepared and go early as there are hundreds of thousands of visitors per day, crowding and sweating in the precious open spaces. In theory, Chatuchak is organised into logical, numbered sections but good luck trying to decipher this while pointy elbows nudge you along. Do some reconnaissance work with Nancy Chandler's *Map of Bangkok,* available at English-language bookshops such as Asia Books (p82).

Be warned that there's no air-conditioning and you'll likely suffer extreme claustrophobia. If dehydration sets in, head towards the clock tower where there is a concentration of cafes or duck outside for a refreshing bowl of *kà·nŏm jeen* (rice noodles with curry sauce). In the evenings, local musicians serenade the crowds who are capping off their shopping spree with happy hour.

OLIVER STREWE / LONELY PLANET IMAGES ©

>9 JIM THOMPSON'S HOUSE

WHAT EXPATS REALLY WANT: THE THAI DREAM HOME

Every foreign visitor who pads around Jim Thompson's House (p80) secretly wishes to live here for a day or more. The former resident was one of Bangkok's most famous expats and used his home as a repository for ageing Thai traditions and artwork. As old wooden houses were falling derelict, Thompson salvaged six teak houses (reputedly built without nails) and assembled them on the banks of Khlong Saen Saeb on an astrologically auspicious date in 1959.

The rooms are adorned with his art collection and personal possessions, including rare Chinese porcelain pieces and Burmese, Cambodian and Thai artefacts, and the tropical garden is punctuated by lush plantings and lotus ponds.

American-born Thompson was an intriguing chap in both life and death. He served in Thailand during WWII and soon returned to Bangkok after finding his home town of New York City a tad too quiet. During his tenure in the City of Angels (as Bangkok is known), he helped revive the Thai cottage industry of handwoven silk, a tradition losing favour domestically. He sent samples of his neighbours' textiles to European fashion houses, resulting in a silk business that continues to this day. His charmed life came to a dramatic end when he vanished during an afternoon stroll in Malaysia's Cameron Highlands in 1967.

MICK ELMORE / LONELY PLANET IMAGES ©

>10 MBK

SHOP LIKE A THAI TEEN AT BANGKOK'S BUSIEST MALL

Forget everything you know about shopping malls and prepare to be wowed by MBK (Mah Boon Krong; p84). Nearly all of the city's population under 20 can be found here on a more regular basis than they can in class or at home. It's the social nexus of the city, with down-to-earth market sensibilities and refreshing air-conditioning.

MBK's main event is the people-watching: grandmas step nervously onto the escalators and hip teenagers cluster into tight cliques. Need a custom-made girdle, mantelpiece painting of you and your dog, or what about some name cards? Probably not, but these are strapping businesses in MBK.

There are of course many irresistible tourist bargains in this everyman mall. Contact lenses, mobile phones and cut-rate fashions are primary draws, along with every permutation of fast-food franchise. Even though it's a Pizza Hut, it's still a distinctly Thai experience: Thais put ketchup on their pizza, and KFC invented its own version of East–West fusion with 'cheezy fries', French fries dipped in melted cheese and then puffed rice (surprisingly delicious).

No visit to MBK is complete without sucking down some sugary drinks, picking up some new zits and catching a movie at the top-floor cinema. This is the Thai teen life you never had.

GREG ELMS / LONELY PLANET IMAGES ©

>BANGKOK DIARY

There's always something going on in Bangkok – be it an international festival sponsored by foreign cultural centres or a national holiday honouring the monarchy. In addition to the cultural and religious events listed here, the city's galleries host opening-exhibition parties and Bangkok's bars and restaurants have adopted any foreign holiday that requires a celebratory drink. The city celebrates no fewer than three New Year's (international, Thai and Chinese). Check the websites of TAT (www.tourismthailand.org) or Bangkok Tourist Division (www.bangkoktourist.com) for festival dates, as they vary. Also check the listings magazines *BK* (www.bkmagazine.com) and *Bangkok 101* (www.bangkok101.com) for city events.

Fire for the guardian spirit of water, Loi Krathong (p29)

FEBRUARY

Chinese New Year

Thai-Chinese celebrate the lunar New Year, with house cleaning, lion dances and fireworks in Chinatown. Occasionally this holiday occurs in March.

APRIL

Songkran

Bangkok's wildest festival, Songkran is a celebration of the Thai lunar New Year involving water throwing. Once a subdued affair, the celebration has devolved into a citywide water fight. Foreigners, especially well-dressed ones, are obvious targets for mischievous locals. The majority of the mayhem occurs on Th Khao San.

MAY

Visakha Bucha

Buddha's birth, enlightenment and passing away are honoured with candlelit processions and other merit-making activities on this religious holiday. Wat Benchamabophit (p69) is well known for its evening rituals.

Decked out to ring in Chinese New Year

KRAIG LIEB / LONELY PLANET IMAGES ©

RICHARD I'ANSON / LONELY PLANET IMAGES ©

If you can't beat 'em, join 'em. Passers-by targeted by water pistol–wielding revellers during Songkran

OCTOBER

Vegetarian Festival

This 10-day Chinese-Buddhist festival requires the devout to purify minds and bodies by abstaining from meat. It is primarily observed in Chinatown, with vendors preparing meatless meals. Just look for the yellow banners to denote vegetarian observation.

Ork Phansa

This marks the end of the wet season and Buddhist Lent. Buddhists typically attend temples to listen to sermons and to prom-enade around the temple three times.

NOVEMBER

Loi Krathong

Thailand's most striking festival, Loi Kra-thong honours the guardian spirit of water with small lotus-shaped boats containing a lit candle that are set adrift on Mae Nam Chao Phraya or other water sources. It is said that couples who float a *kràthong* (ceremo-nial float) together will never drift apart. Because this is a lunar festival, sometimes it falls in October.

It's my party: the king surveys the honour guard at his birthday parade

MICK ELMORE / LONELY PLANET IMAGES ©

DECEMBER

HM King's Birthday

The country's revered monarchy is honoured on the king's birthday (5 December) with household decorations and twinkling lights placed around Bangkok's Grand Palace. This day is also recognised as 'Father's Day' and provides many city workers an opportunity to travel home to the provinces.

New Year's Eve

Fireworks and festivities take place across the city in honour of the international New Year.

>ITINERARIES

The monumental beauty of Wat Arun (p44) never ceases to amaze

ITINERARIES

Just getting around Bangkok is a mental and physical work
and humidity are withering, and the city layout confoundin~~ible
with your expectations and leave room for snacking and wandering. During these unplanned outings you'll stumble on Bangkok's best sights: kids
playing badminton, street-corner gossip sessions and open-air kitchens.

DAY ONE

Get up early in the morning to watch the silent promenade of monks
on their alms route, collecting the day's sustenance from housewives
and shopkeepers. Banglamphu is the best neighbourhood to watch
this ritual. Then head over to the Grand Palace and Wat Phra Kaew (p10)
before the day gets too hot and the crowds too thick. Afterwards, stroll
over to Wat Pho (p14) and hop across the river to Wat Arun (p44). That's
enough temple-spotting for one day. Catch a river express boat back to
Banglamphu for lunch at Roti-Mataba (p60) and wander along Th Phra
Athit and into the backpackers ghetto around Th Khao San. Sup at Poj
Spa Kar (p59) and imbibe at the streetside bars on Th Khao San (p61).

DAY TWO

If you're primed for more heat and crowds, head to Chinatown (p16) and
wander the fresh-food and hardware markets for shopping voyeurism.
Stop into the various temples or just poke around the streamlike *soi* (lanes)
that will render you thoroughly lost – the only way to explore this neighbourhood. Afterwards, you'll need a sensory soother with a visit to peaceful
Jim Thompson's House (p25), a tranquil collection of antique architecture
and art. If you're a glutton for punishment or just a glutton for good food,
return to Chinatown once the sun sets for a streetside seafood feast (p77).
Wrap up the evening with a nightcap at a sky-high bar (see p106) that
drinks in the twinkling lights and ambient roar of the city below.

DAY THREE

If it's a weekend, take the BTS train all the way to the northernmost stop
to the mammoth Chatuchak Weekend Market (p24), which will consume

---

Top Sip a cocktail and enjoy the high life at Sirocco & Sky Bar (p106) **Bottom** Thai cuisine: a delectable fusion of colour and flavour (p158)

a whole day with shopping, bargaining and sweating. Combat the temperature with lots of treats at the market's makeshift cafes. Arrive early in the morning to beat the heat and the crowds and give yourself a late-day siesta. Then head out to catch some upscale Thai food at nahm (p111), quite possibly Bangkok's best Thai restaurant. After searing your taste buds with the famously spicy cuisine, polish off the night with a visit to some of Bangkok's international-strength clubs, such as Bed Supperclub (p130) or 808 Club (p142). The crowds are fickle at these late-night playgrounds so watch the press – try the Bangkok Recorder (www.bangkok recorder.com) – for visiting DJs or popular theme nights.

BANGKOK HAVEN

Whether pouring rain or boiling hot, Bangkok is sometimes best viewed from inside an air-conditioned building. If you've landed during the wet season, keep in mind that the monsoons usually strike in the late afternoon and can make catching a cab almost impossible. Seek shelter in the comfortable cocoon of the city's various shopping centres. For a city that resists planning, the shopping centres have managed to proliferate around Siam Square and have spread into covered walkways leading directly to the BTS stations so that fragile fashionistas are protected from the elements. First stop is Bangkok's largest mall, Siam Paragon (p86); then on to Siam Center and Siam Discovery Center (p86) for books, fashion and design products. But leave most of the day for MBK (p26), which is like an Asian-style market brought indoors. Grab lunch or dinner at one of the mall's food courts, all of which serve up tasty market-style dishes in air-conditioned comfort. After a day of hiding from the elements, enjoy the cooler temperatures of nightfall at the circus of Patpong (p99) and the nearby bars and clubs.

REJUVENATING BANGKOK

There is a peaceful side to this chaotic city – after all, most residents pass their time in traffic by meditating. Bangkok's quieter attractions include pretty Dusit Palace Park (p22), where the monarchy built a Thai version of the ornamental Victorian era. Or climb up to the breezy viewpoint from Wat Saket's Golden Mount (p54) and breathe in the fresh air against a skyline of temple spires. Prolong your serenity with a visit to a day spa, such as Divana Massage & Spa (p119), which is set in a charming garden enclave, a common feature when Th Sukhumvit was an avenue of the well-to-do. If you're pressed for time, enjoy a straightforward body massage at Ruen-Nuad Massage Studio (p97), which partakes of an equally Thai but simpler setting. A day of relaxation can be rewarded with an evening of gastronomy. Bo.lan (p125) is that rare Bangkok restaurant that stays true to Thai flavours in a stylish setting. Finish off the night amid the old-world charm of the Oriental Hotel's Bamboo Bar (p106).

NIGHT-OWL BANGKOK

If your nights are your days, Bangkok is still an entertaining host. In days past, this city was more wild and free-spirited, but the partygoers are a tenacious lot, circumventing city rules with teenage bravado. Bars on and around Th Khao San (p61) rock out every night and continue the party on the streets after closing time. Although Th Khao San is the backpacker ghetto, young Thais are claiming it as a hip scene for indie bands. If you're more of a DJ club butterfly, trek out to Ekamai Soi 5 (p131) or RCA (p142), where you can pick and choose from a smorgasbord of warehouse-sized clubs. After 2am, grab a meal at Soi 38 Night Market (p128) to stave off a hangover. If you're not in bed before daybreak, head to Banglamphu to watch the monks on their morning alms rounds.

FORWARD PLANNING

It may come as a surprise that Bangkok doesn't require a lot of advance booking. Except for flights and a first-night reservation, you could literally step off the plane and survive swimmingly.

Three weeks before you go Watch the web, especially www.asia-hotels.com, for hotel promotions and discounts. Read up on Thai culture and etiquette with the books *Very Thai: Everyday Pop Culture* by Philip Cornwel-Smith and *Culture Shock! Thailand* by Robert and Nanthapa Cooper. Start following Bangkok news at 2Bangkok.com or the online sites of the English-language newspapers, such as *Bangkok Post* (www.bangkokpost.com) and the *Nation* (www.nationmultimedia.com).

One week before you go Ditch those spaghetti-strap tops for something flouncy and urban but with less décolletage. Peruse Lonely Planet's Thorntree (http://thorntree.lonelyplanet.com) for tips on avoiding Bangkok's many scams, such as dodgy túk-túks or bogus gem and tailor shops.

The day before you go Stay out all night so that you'll sleep on the flight. Hang out in a sauna for weather acclimation. Say bon voyage to your favourite bread and cheese, as Bangkok is still on a rice diet. Start dreaming about Thai curries by visiting the food blog at www.austinbushphotography.com/category/foodblog.

GREG ELMS / LONELY PLANET IMAGES ©
Chitchatting: the unofficial national pastime

NEIGHBOURHOODS

Bangkok is the 'capital' in every sense of the word. It is Thailand's commercial, creative, economic and consuming centre, attracting rural villagers saddled with debt, globetrotting expats managing multinationals, bilingual high-society types, hip spendthrift teens and small-time import-exporters in the city's ethnic enclaves.

Half the fun of 'seeing' Bangkok is getting there – no small task. Bangkok sprawls as impetuously as its most prominent landmark, Mae Nam Chao Phraya (Chao Phraya River). The more predictable railway line heading north from Hualamphong train station neatly divides the central city area into old and new Bangkok.

Old Bangkok cradles Ko Ratanakosin, the original royal district filled with historic monuments. Following the river north is charming Banglamphu, a residential neighbourhood of shophouses and the backpacker spectacle of Th Khao San. Sitting astride Banglamphu like a mahout is Dusit, home to Vimanmek teak mansion and the royal residence, Chitlada Palace.

Either side of Hualamphong station is bustling Chinatown; the outer western ring is known as Phahurat (Little India). Further south is the area we define as Riverside, sprinkled with crumbling colonial-style buildings and grand churches.

Newer Bangkok is centred on Silom, Sukhumvit and Siam Square, crammed with skyscrapers, traffic and neon lights. Th Silom is a clogged artery that connects the river to the southern boundary of Lumphini Park and boasts infamous Patpong. Another boundary is Th Witthayu and Soi Lang Suan, the workplace and playground for the diplomatic corps.

Credit-card addicts and fashion-obsessed teenagers leapfrog between shopping centres in the Siam Square area surrounding Th Phra Ram I.

Following Th Phra Ram I east leads to Th Sukhumvit. This is the executive-expat address, where satellite communities of foreigners ease homesickness with visits to restaurants specialising in their respective national dishes.

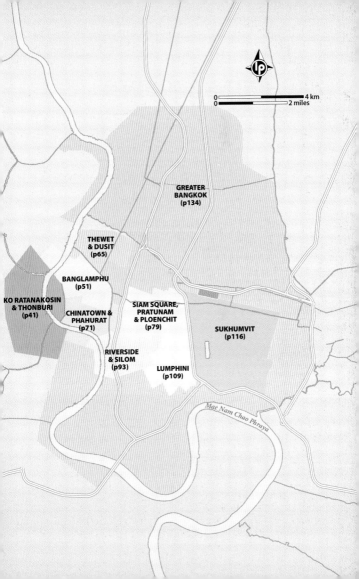

GREATER
BANGKOK
(p134)

THEWET
& DUSIT
(p65)

BANGLAMPHU
(p51)

KO RATANAKOSIN
& THONBURI
(p41)

CHINATOWN &
PHAHURAT
(p71)

SIAM SQUARE,
PRATUNAM
& PLOENCHIT
(p79)

SUKHUMVIT
(p116)

RIVERSIDE
& SILOM
(p93)

LUMPHINI
(p109)

Mae Nam Chao Phraya

0 ━━━━━ 4 km
0 ━━━━━ 2 miles

>KO RATANAKOSIN & THONBURI

The first stop for all sightseers, Ko Ratanakosin was the royal centre of Bangkok until the turn of the 20th century. Bounded by both the river and man-made canals, this island district contains important palaces and temples, showcasing Thailand's peculiar marriage of monarchy and religion. More monuments to Thailand's history are found directly across the river in Thonburi, which served briefly as the capital until it was replaced by Bangkok.

Cultural attractions will dominate your visit here, but the street life will be the ultimate charm. Come early in the morning, before the sun and the crowds reach maximum strength, and stroll the pavements of Th Maha Rat past the crumbling neoclassical warehouses and small medicine shops.

Beware, though – rip-off artists prowl this tourist area. Ignore any stranger who approaches you about an attraction being closed.

KO RATANAKOSIN & THONBURI

👁 SEE
Church of Santa Cruz 1 C6
Grand Palace 2 C3
Lak Meuang 3 C3
Museum of Siam 4 C5
National Museum 5 C1
Royal Barges National
 Museum 6 A1
Sanam Luang 7 C2
Songkran Niyosane
 Forensic Museum 8 B1
Wat Arun 9 B5
Wat Mahathat 10 C2
Wat Pho 11 C4
Wat Phra Kaew 12 C3

🏃 DO
Segway Tour Thailand ..13 B2
Wat Mahathat's
 International Buddhist
 Meditation Centre ... (see 10)
Wat Pho Thai
 Traditional Medical
 & Massage School 14 C5

🛍 SHOP
Amulet Market 15 B2

🍴 EAT
Khunkung 16 B3
Rub Aroon 17 C4

🍸 DRINK
Amorosa 18 C4

⭐ PLAY
National Theatre 19 C1
Patravadi Theatre 20 B3

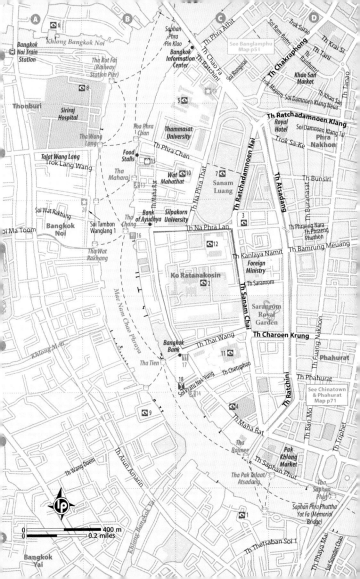

👁 SEE

👁 GRAND PALACE & WAT PHRA KAEW

☎ 0 2224 1833; www.palaces.thai.
net; Th Na Phra Lan; admission 350B;
🕑 8.30am-3.30pm; 🚌 25, 32, 503, 508,
🚤 Tha Chang

There is no other site in Thailand more holy or more famous than Wat Phra Kaew (Temple of the Emerald Buddha) and the attached Grand Palace, the former royal residence. For more information on these sights, see p10. A strict dress code is enforced; see the boxed text on p44. The admission price to the Grand Palace and Wat Phra Kaew includes free entrance to Dusit Palace Park (p67).

👁 LAK MEUANG

cnr Th Ratchadamnoen Nai & Th Lak
Meuang; admission free; 🕑 6.30am-
6.30pm; 🚌 2, 60, 507, 🚤 Tha Chang; ♿

A wooden pillar containing the city guardian (Lak Meuang) is housed in this shrine, at the southeastern corner of Sanam Luang. The pillar was placed here at the founding of the new capital and today worshippers come and make offerings by commissioning traditional dances or delivering severed pigs' heads decorated with incense.

👁 MUSEUM OF SIAM

☎ 0 2225 2777; www.museumsiam.
com; Th Maha Rat; admission 300B;
🕑 10am-6pm Tue-Sun; 🚌 32, 524,
🚤 Tha Tien

Guardian devils at Wat Arun (p44)

GREG ELMS / LONELY PLANET IMAGES ©

This museum employs a variety of media to explore the origins of the Thai people and their culture. The exhibits are interactive, well balanced and entertaining; highlights include the informative and engaging narrated videos in each exhibition room and an interactive Ayuthaya-era battle game.

🄯 NATIONAL MUSEUM

☎ 0 2224 1402; Th Na Phra That; admission 200B; ⏱ 9am-3.30pm Wed-Sun, free tours 9.30am Wed & Thu; 🚌 32, 123, 503, 🚢 Tha Chang; ♿

One of the region's best collections of Buddha images resides in this unassuming museum of art and history. Come for the weekly tours to gain a better appreciation of the undersigned exhibits.

🄯 ROYAL BARGES NATIONAL MUSEUM

☎ 0 2424 0004; Khlong Bangkok Noi, Thonburi; admission 100B (200B to take photos); ⏱ 9am-5pm; 🚢 Tha Saphan Phra Pin Klao, then walk or taxi

For ceremonial occasions, the elaborately carved barges at this museum are dusted off for a grand riverine procession. The bows' figureheads depict such Hindu gods as *garuda* (eagle-man and Vishnu's mount), *naga* (multiheaded sea serpent) and *supphannahong* (golden swan). The *Supphannahong* boat traditionally carries the king and is the world's largest dugout.

PARTING THE WATERS

Dating back to the days of the Ayuthaya court, a royal outing meant a barge procession: hundreds of men rowing sleek, gold-covered boats accompanied by rhythm-makers and royal chanters. In modern times, the elaborate procession is infrequently staged during the *gà-tĭn* ceremony (when robes are offered to monks in a merit-making ritual) or during important anniversaries. The most recent staging of this colourful event was in 2006 to honour the king's 60th year on the throne.

🄯 SANAM LUANG

bordered by Th Na Phra That, Th Na Phra Lan, Th Ratchadamnoen Nai, Th Somdet Phra Pin Klao; admission free; ⏱ 5am-8pm; 🚌 32, 123, 503, 🚢 Tha Chang; ♿

Lumphini Park may be the green heart of Bangkok but Sanam Luang (Royal Field) is its ceremonial soul. Cremations of members of the royal family and the annual May ploughing ceremony, which kicks off the rice-growing season, are held here.

🄯 SONGKRAN NIYOSANE FORENSIC MUSEUM

☎ 0 2419 7000; 2nd fl, Forensic Pathology Bldg, Siriraj Hospital, Th Phrannok, Thonburi; admission 40B; ⏱ 8.30am-4.30pm Mon-Fri; 🚢 Tha Wang Lang

Seriously, do not come to this museum with a full stomach. On

43

NEIGHBOURHOODS

KO RATANAKOSIN & THONBURI

DRESS FOR THE OCCASION

Most of Bangkok's biggest tourist attractions are in fact sacred places, and visitors should dress and behave appropriately. In particular, at Wat Phra Kaew, the Grand Palace and in Dusit Palace Park, you won't be allowed to enter unless you're well covered. Shorts, sleeveless shirts or spaghetti-strap tops, capri pants – basically anything that reveals more than your arms (not your shoulders) and head – are not allowed. This applies to men and women. Those who aren't dressed appropriately can expect to be shown into a dressing room and issued with a sarong before being allowed in. For walking in the courtyard areas you are supposed to wear shoes with closed heels and toes, although these rules aren't as zealously enforced. Regardless, footwear should always be removed before entering any main *bòht* (chapel) or *wí-hähn* (sanctuary). When sitting in front of a Buddha image, tuck your feet behind you to avoid the highly offensive pose of pointing your feet towards a revered figure.

display are preserved body parts that have been crushed, shot, stabbed and raped, with grisly before-and-after photos, as well as the entire remains of a notorious Thai murderer.

◉ WAT ARUN

☎ Th Arun Amarin, Thonburi; admission 50B, cross-river ferry 3.50B; ⏰ 8.30am-5.30pm; ⛴ cross-river ferry from Tha Tien

The precursor to modern skyscrapers, this Khmer-style temple dominates the river landscape like an ancient military installation. Up close, the masculine monument is decorated in delicate mosaic details and marks the re-emergence of the Thai capital after the Burmese invasion in the 18th century.

◉ WAT MAHATHAT

☎ 0 2223 6878; 3 Th Maha Rat; admission free; ⏰ 9am-5pm; 🚌 32, 201, 503, ⛴ Tha Maharaj or Tha Chang

The centre of learning for the Mahanikai sect of Buddhist monks, Wat Mahathat is a workaday temple lacking in red-carpet appeal. Instead, come to take part in the ordinary life of a Thai temple: making merit or studying meditation. For more information on Wat Mahathat, see p18.

◉ WAT PHO

☎ 0 2225 9595; www.watpho.com; Th Chetuphon & Th Sanam Chai; admission 50B; ⏰ 8am-9pm; 🚌 123, 508, ⛴ Tha Tien; ♿

Second on the tourist itinerary after Wat Phra Kaew, Wat Pho has many more curious corners (and massage pavilions) to explore beyond the crowd-pleasing Buddha,

Prasuputh Chainikom (Kosalo)
Meditation master at Wat Mahathat

Why did you become a monk? I can develop my own life and help other people. **Why teach foreigners?** I have English skills and experience with meditation – most Thai monks don't have these skills. **Why are so many foreigners interested in meditation?** We're all stressed. Meditation teaches us how to relax our minds. If we know how to relax, we can find peace. **Can one study meditation if one is not Buddhist or has no experience?** Yes. When we practise meditation, we're not thinking of the Buddha, we're just trying to make our minds empty. **What benefits does meditation provide?** 1. It purifies your mind. 2. It gets rid of sorrow and lamentation. 3. It gets rid of physical and mental suffering. 4. It helps us understand the truth of life. 5. You can extinguish suffering and attain nirvana. Five is difficult, but if you try, you can attain one to four.

a 46m-long and 15m-high figure illustrating Buddha's passing into nirvana. It is also home to the largest collection of Buddha images in the country and the earliest centre for public education. For more information on the temple complex, see p14.

🏃 DO

🏃 SEGWAY TOUR THAILAND
Segway Tours
☎ 0 2221 4525; www.segwaytourthailand.com; Maharaj Pier Bldg, Tha Maharaj, off Th Maha Rat; tours from 3500B; ⏲ 9.30am-6.30pm Tue-Sun; 🚌 32, 201, 503, ⚓ Tha Maharaj or Tha Chang
Bicycles are so 20th century; explore Bangkok from the, er, platform of an electronic Segway. This new outfit runs half-day and full-day Segway tours in and around Bangkok, including excursions among the ruins in Ayuthaya.

🏃 WAT MAHATHAT'S INTERNATIONAL BUDDHIST MEDITATION CENTRE *Meditation*
☎ 0 2222 6011; Section 5, Wat Mahathat, 3 Th Maha Rat; donations accepted; ⏲ 7am, 1pm & 6pm; 🚌 32, 201, 503, ⚓ Tha Maharaj or Tha Chang
The International Buddhist Meditation Centre at Wat Mahathat is where most Westerners study *satipatthana* (mindful meditation) in Bangkok. Classes last three hours and participants are welcome to join the meditation periods or adhere to a more strict immersion into temple life with residential courses.

🏃 WAT PHO THAI TRADITIONAL MEDICAL & MASSAGE SCHOOL *Massage*
☎ 0 2622 3550; www.watpomassage.com; Soi Penphat; ⏲ 8am-6pm; 🚌 123, 508, ⚓ Tha Tien; ♿
The primary training school for Thai massage also has an air-

---

WORTH THE TRIP
When Bangkok was a port of call, Western nations sailed in to stake a claim in the lucrative Asia sea trade. Located around the Oriental Hotel were the headquarters of shipping interests, the French embassy and Christian churches. The biggest church-builders were the Portuguese, some of the first Europeans in the kingdom (due in part to their nearby colony of Malacca in Malaysia). They were given prime riverside real estate in recognition for their contribution in securing the new capital after the fall of Ayuthaya. The surviving churches, **Holy Rosary Church** (Map p93, B1; Th Yotha; ⏲ 8am-5pm) and **Church of Santa Cruz** (Soi Kuti Jiin, Thonburi; ⏲ 7am-4pm), are still in operation and boast parishes of many former Indochinese citizens.

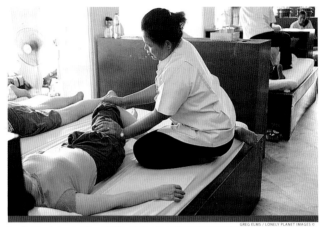

GREG ELMS / LONELY PLANET IMAGES ©

Learning the art of manipulation at Wat Pho Thai Traditional Medical & Massage School

conditioned drop-in centre for exhausted sightseers needing a little kneading. If impressed by their work, you might consider enrolling in one of the multiday classes on different aspects of this traditional art. There are also massage pavilions on the temple grounds. Soi Penphat is not signed; look for the *soi* with Coconut Palm restaurant.

🛍 SHOP

🛍 AMULET MARKET *Market*
Th Maha Rat; ⏱ 7am-5pm; 🚌 32, 201, 503, 🚢 Tha Maharaj or Tha Chang
If you need a charm to stop bullets or even a set of pre-owned

dentures, wander through this streetside market catering to fate and fortune and the ability to alter the two. The amulet market begins on the sidewalks of Th Maha Rat and follows the narrow *soi* (lanes) that lead to the river. For more information, see p18.

🍴 EAT

🍴 KHUNKUNG *Thai* $$
Tha Chang; ⏱ 11am-2pm & 4-10pm Mon-Fri, 11am-10pm Sat & Sun; 🚌 25, 32, 503, 508, 🚢 Tha Chang; ♿
This cafeteria-like restaurant located in the compound of the Royal Navy Association has one of the few coveted riverfront

locations along this stretch of the Mae Nam Chao Phraya. Locals come for cheap and tasty seafood-based eats such as fried rice with crab, or semidried cottonfish served with a sour mango dressing. The entrance to the restaurant is near the ATMs at Tha Chang.

🍴 RUB AROON *Thai*　　　$$
Th Maha Rat; ⏰ **8am-6pm;** 🚌 **123, 508,** 🚢 **Tha Tien;** ♿ 👶 Ⓥ
This traveller-friendly cafe is a pleasant escape from sightseeing in Ko Ratanakosin. The restored shopfront opens directly out to the street and there is cosy seating and patient service. The dishes are basic and delicious, served alongside fruit drinks and coffees for sipping away tropical fatigue.

🍸 DRINK

🍸 AMOROSA *Bar*
☎ **0 2221 9158; www.arunresidence.com;
Arun Residence, 36-38 Soi Pratu Nok Yung;**
⏰ **6-11pm;** 🚌 **123, 508,** 🚢 **Tha Tien**
It may be the only bar in the area, but that doesn't mean it's any sort of compromise. Amorosa's rooftop location packs killer views of Wat Arun, making it one of the best spots in Bangkok for a riverside sundowner.

⭐ PLAY

⭐ NATIONAL THEATRE *Theatre*
☎ **0 2224 1342; 2 Th Ratchini; tickets 60-
100B;** 🚌 **32, 123, 503,** 🚢 **Tha Chang;** 👶
After a lengthy renovation, the National Theatre is again open for business. Performances of *khon,* masked dance-drama often depicting scenes from the

---

FREE RIDE

Launched in 2008, **Bangkok Smile Bike** is a municipally sponsored program encouraging visitors to explore parts of old Bangkok and Thonburi by bicycle. The small green bikes can be borrowed for free, and an expansive tourist route encompassing the areas' major sites has been marked by relatively clear road signs and occasional green bike lanes. There are five stations spread out between Ko Ratanakosin and Banglamphu, and the suggested starting/ending point is at the southwest corner of **Sanam Luang** (p43), across from the main entrance to the Grand Palace and Wat Phra Kaew. On the Thonburi side, there are six stations and the suggested starting point is at the base of Saphan Phra Pin Klao, with the route ending at Saphan Phra Phuttha Yot Fa (Memorial Bridge). Bikes are available from 10am to 5pm, and you'll need some form of ID to borrow one.

NEIGHBOURHOODS

MURAL MASTERS

Thailand's real artistic treasures aren't hung on gallery walls but rather appear as temple murals painted by largely anonymous visual storytellers. Temple murals were used to beautify interiors and explain the story of Buddha and his past lives *(Jataka)* to a largely illiterate populace. In the corners of these busy painted stages are elements of everyday life – housewives fetching water and fishermen mending nets. Some stunning examples of these visual sermons can be found at **Wat Chong Nonsi** (off Map p134; Th Nonsi; 🕑 8.30am-6pm), which has rare unrenovated Ayuthaya-era murals; and **Wat Suwannaram** (off Map p134; Khlong Bangkok Noi; 🕑 9am-6pm), boasting murals by two pre-eminent artists of the Rama III era. Beginning mural-spotters usually start with **Wat Phra Kaew** (p42) and **Wat Suthat** (p54).

Ramayana, are held on the first and second Sundays of the month. *Lá·kon* (Thai dance-dramas) are held on the first Friday of the month, and Thai musical performances are held on the third Friday of the month.

⭐ **PATRAVADI THEATRE** *Theatre*
☎ 0 2412 7287; www.patravaditheatre.com; Soi Tambon Wanglang 1, Thonburi;

tickets 300-800B; 🕑 schedule varies; 🚢 private cross-river ferry from Tha Maharaj; ♿

Patravadi is Bangkok's only open-air theatre and one of its most avant garde. Led by Patravadi Mejudhon, a famous Thai actor and playwright, the troupe's performances blend traditional Thai dance with modern choreography, music and costume.

KO RATANAKOSIN & THONBURI

>BANGLAMPHU

Easily Bangkok's most charming neighbourhood, Banglamphu is the city's former aristocratic enclave, once filled with minor royalty and riverside mansions. Today the old quarter is dominated by backpackers seeking R&R on famous Th Khao San, civil servants sauntering between offices and lunch spots, and Bangkok's only enclave of bohemian artists and students.

In Banglamphu, trees still outnumber high-rises, and monks make their morning alms route often before the backpackers have heard last call. The travellers' amenities are thick and cheap in this neighbourhood: you'll find loads of souvenir shopping and late-night imbibing. On the edges of the tourist zone there's a maze of two-storey shophouses, each decorated with terracotta water gardens or potted plants and low-hanging shades that block out the mean sun. Vendor carts are plentiful in this area, so is people-watching and unfettered wandering. To catch a better glimpse into daily Thai life, wander the *soi* (lanes) that branch off Th Samsen on the northern side of Khlong Banglamphu, or check out the nationalistic paraphernalia shops on Th Phra Sumen.

BANGLAMPHU

◎ SEE

The gateway to Banglamphu is along Th Ratchadamnoen Klang, a wide European-style boulevard lined with billboard-sized pictures of the king and the royal family. The showcase attractions along the royal boulevard are beautifully lit at night, giving the illusion of a picture-book fantasy of the exotic East.

◎ DEMOCRACY MONUMENT

cnr Th Ratchadamnoen Klang & Th Din So; admission free; 🚌 2, 15, 44, 511, 🚤 khlong taxi to Tha Phan Fah

Four-pronged Democracy Monument holds a key place in Bangkok's political history. Built to commemorate the nation's transition from absolute monarchy to constitutional monarchy in 1932, the monument is the natural home of pro-democracy rallies, including the tragic demonstrations of 1992 that turned bloody.

◎ NATIONAL GALLERY

☎ 0 2281 2224; 4 Th Chao Fa; admission 200B; 🕙 9am-4pm Wed-Sun; 🚤 Tha Phra Athit; ♿

Based in the old mint building, this government-funded museum has a very subdued collection of traditional and contemporary art. The general opinion is that this is not the best pedestal for Thailand's artistic traditions, but it is rarely crowded and is comfortably air-conditioned.

◎ QUEEN'S GALLERY

☎ 0 2281 5360; www.queengallery.org; 101 Th Ratchadamnoen Klang; admission 30B; 🕙 10am-7pm Thu-Tue; 🚌 2, 15, 44, 511, 🚤 khlong taxi to Tha Phan Fah

A project funded by the queen, this museum presents paintings and sculpture by renowned domestic and international artists. Most Thai artists featured at the Queen's Gallery have been recognised as National Artists or receive

---

LET ME BE YOUR GUIDE

If you require a bit of guidance around Bangkok's sights, recommended outfits include **Tour with Tong** (🕙 0 81835 0240; www.tourwithtong.com; day tours from 1000B), whose team conducts tours in and around Bangkok, and **Thai Private Tour Guide** (🕙 0 81860 9159; www.thaitourguide.com; day tours from 2000B), where Chob and Mee get good reviews. For something that is a bit more specific, **Bangkok Private Tours** (www.bangkokprivate tours.com; full-day walking tours 3400B) conducts customised walking tours of the city, while foodies can opt for **Bangkok Food Tours** (🕙 0 89126 3657; www.bangkokfood tours.com; half-day tours 950/750B), which offers half-day culinary tours of Bangkok's Bang Rak neighbourhood.

> **BELOVED CROWN & COUNTRY**
> The king, nation and religion are indescribably linked in Thailand, but a walk along Th Phra Sumen can help illustrate it. Start at Wat Bowonniwet, which is the 'royal' temple: it and the affiliated Thammayut reformation sect were founded by Rama IV (King Mongkut), who served as the temple's first abbot. Rama IV was a scholar before a monarch and wished to expunge some of the superstitious elements from Thai Buddhism. Successive kings have been ordained here and the sect continues a close relationship with the crown. The temple itself betrays little of this connection but the nearby shophouses heading east towards Th Prachathipatai sell full-size pictures of the king, national and religious flags, and other paraphernalia of the Thai triumvirate.

funding through the queen's Support foundation for the preservation of handicrafts.

◙ SANTICHAIPRAKAN PARK & PHRA SUMEN FORT
cnr Th Phra Athit; admission free; 5am-8pm; 32, 33, 64, 82, Tha Phra Athit;

It's a tiny patch of greenery with a great river view and lots of evening action, including comical communal aerobics classes. The riverside pathway heading southwards makes for a serene promenade. The park's most prominent landmark is the blindingly white Phra Sumen Fort, which was built in 1783 to defend the city against a river invasion.

◙ WAT BOWONNIWET
cnr Th Phra Sumen & Th Tanao; donations accepted; 8am-5.30pm; 56, 58, 516, Tha Phra Athit;

Home to the Buddhist Mahamakut University, this royally affiliated monastery is the national headquarters of the Thammayut sect of Thai Buddhism. It may be in ultra-casual Banglamphu but it's also where the present king was ordained. Visitors must dress appropriately.

◙ WAT RATCHANATDARAM WORAWIHAN
cnr Th Ratchadamnoen Klang & Th Mahachai; donations accepted; 9am-5pm; 2, 15, 44, 511, khlong taxi to Tha Phan Fah

Across Th Mahachai from Wat Saket, Wat Ratchanatdaram was built for Rama III's granddaughter. Today this temple is better known for Loha Prasat, the metallic, castlelike monastery, with many passageways and meditation cells at each intersection, as well as a busy amulet market.

 WAT SAKET & GOLDEN MOUNT

Th Boriphat; admission 10B; 🕐 7.30am-5.30pm; 🚌 8, 37, 47, 🚤 khlong taxi to Tha Phan Fah

A less conspicuous member of the temple itinerary, the Golden Mount is an artificial hill from which Bangkok appears meditatively serene. Next door, Wat Saket has some interesting Buddhist murals. Join the candlelit procession to the summit in November during the temple fair.

WAT SUTHAT & GIANT SWING

Th Bamrung Meuang; admission 20B; 🕐 8.30am-9pm; 🚌 10, 12, 🚤 khlong taxi to Tha Phan Fah

Wat Suthat holds the highest royal temple grade. Inside the *wí·hǎhn* (sanctuary for a Buddha sculpture) are intricate *Jataka* (stories of the Buddha) murals and Thailand's biggest surviving Sukhothai-era bronze Buddha. Over the road is the Giant Swing (Sao Ching-Cha), site of a former Brahman festival in honour of Shiva.

DO

GRASSHOPPER ADVENTURES *Bicycle Tours*

☎ 0 2280 0832; www.grasshopper adventures.com; 57 Th Ratchadamnoen Klang; 🕐 8.30am-6.30pm Mon-Fri; 🚌 2, 15, 44, 511, 🚤 khlong taxi to Tha Phan Fah

Lost baggage? Buy an entire wardrobe at the markets on Th Khao San

GREG ELMS / LONELY PLANET IMAGES ©

DRIVING A HARD BARGAIN

Thais respect a good bargainer, someone who can get a reasonable price without either seller or buyer losing face. Here are some hints:

> Do your homework on prices
> Don't start bargaining unless you intend to buy
> Always let the vendor make the first offer and then ask, 'Can you discount the price?'
> Don't be aggressive or raise your voice; be friendly
> Remember that there's a fine line between bargaining and niggling; it is considered poor form to argue over 10B

This lauded outfit runs a variety of unique bicycle tours in and around Bangkok, including a night tour and a tour of the city's green zones.

🏃 KHAO *Cooking School*
☎ 0 89111 0947; www.khaocooking school.com; D&D Plaza, 68-70 Th Khao San; ⏲ classes 9.30am-12.30pm & 1.30-4.30pm; 🚌 32, 516, 🚢 Tha Phra Athit
Although it's located smack dab in the middle of Th Khao San, this tiny cooking school was started up by an authority on Thai food and features instruction on a wide variety of authentic dishes. Located in the courtyard behind D&D Inn.

🏃 SOR VORAPIN GYM *Muay Thai*
☎ 0 2282 3551; www.thaiboxings.com; 13 Th Kasab, Th Chakraphong; 🚌 32, 516, 🚢 Tha Phra Athit
Specialising in training foreign students of both genders, this gym is sweating distance from Th Khao San. More serious training is held at a gym outside the city.

🛍 SHOP

You'll be magnetically drawn to Banglamphu for shopping. Vendors line all of Th Khao San from midmorning to late night selling every possible souvenir and even an evolving selection of funky fashion. This is a bargaining district so don't forget to haggle, which is considered normal procedure if done with a smile and a spirit of goodwill.

🛍 KHAO SAN MARKET *Market*
Th Khao San; ⏲ 10am-11pm Tue-Sun; 🚌 2, 15, 44, 511, 🚢 Tha Phra Athit; ♿
Got a grubby backpack that needs filling? You'll find gifts and souvenirs that line the Southeast Asia pancake trail: hair-braids, bootleg CDs, Thai knick-knacks and hippy jewellery. At night the selection targets the fashion-conscious Thai teens. The sizes fit more burly folks, the prices are penny-pinching cheap and there's always someone misbehaving.

🏛 MONK'S BOWL VILLAGE
Handicrafts

Soi Ban Baat, off Th Boriphat; 🕐 **10am-8pm;** 🚌 **8, 37, 47,** 🚣 **khlong taxi to Tha Phan Fah**

The only surviving village of three founded by Rama I, Ban Baat (Monk's Bowl Village) still hand-hammers eight pieces of steel (representing Buddha's eightfold path) into the distinctive alms bowls used by monks to receive morning food donations. Tourists instead of temples are the primary patrons these days and a bowl purchase is usually rewarded with a demonstration.

🏛 NITTAYA CURRY SHOP
Cooking Supplies

☎ **0 2282 8212; 136-40 Th Chakraphong;** 🕐 **9am-7pm Mon-Sat;** 🚌 **32, 516,** 🚣 **Tha Phra Athit**

Fresh markets are filled with conical-shaped mountains of curry paste that simplify the dinner routine for many home cooks. If you'd like your own reserve of high-quality paste, step into this neighbourhood curry shop, which sells vacuum-sealed bags of green, red and yellow curry ready to use for post-trip dinner parties. Also check out the snack and gift sections.

🏛 RELIGIOUS SUPPLY SHOPS
Market

Th Bamrung Meuang; 🕐 **10am-7pm Mon-Sat;** 🚌 **10, 12,** 🚣 **khlong taxi to Tha Phan Fah**

Everyone in Bangkok knows that if you need a gigantic bronze Buddha or a miniature model of a monk, this is where you come. The rest of us may have slightly different shopping needs, but this strip of shophouses along Th Bamrung Meuang – itself a former elephant path to the Grand Palace – is Bangkok-style window shopping at its most fascinating and bizarre.

KHLONG TAXI: THE LOCALS' SHORTCUT

Forget about trying to get in or out of Banglamphu during rush hour. Even the military has to contend with the district's clogged arteries: it staged the 2006 coup around midnight, the best time to avoid gridlock. But the locals know that the area's one remaining canal, famously polluted *khlong* Saen Saeb, is a friend indeed during commute time. Even if you're not an office worker, the crafty boats that ply the canal provide a quintessential flight through the City of Angels. (Just remember to cover your face if the boat hits any wake to avoid contact with septic water, and hold on tight when climbing on or off the boat.) You can catch the *khlong* taxi from Tha Phan Fah, near Wat Saket, to reach the Siam Square area (Tha Ratchathewi); boats run from 6am to 7pm and cost from 9B to 21B, depending on the stop.

Handmade alms bowls are the speciality at Monk's Bowl Village

RICHARD I'ANSON / LONELY PLANET IMAGES ©

📖 RIMKHOBFAH BOOKSTORE
Books

☎ 0 2622 3510; 78/1 Th Ratchadamnoen Klang; ⏱ 10am-7pm; 🚌 2, 15, 44, 511, 🛥 khlong taxi to Tha Phan Fah; ♿

For the pseudo nerds among us, this bookstore has plenty of glossy books on Thai arts and culture. Without committing loads of baht, you can sample an array of skinny scholarly publications from the Fine Arts Department on such topics as *What is a Buddha Image?*

📖 TAEKEE TAEKON *Handicrafts*
☎ 0 2629 1473; 118 Th Phra Athit; ⏱ 9am-6pm Mon-Sat; 🚌 32, 33, 64, 82, 🛥 Tha Phra Athit

This shop has a beautiful selection of handwoven textiles from silk-producing regions, especially northern Thailand. If mum won't dig another wooden

elephant, you'll also find a small assortment of classy handicraft souvenirs.

🍴 EAT

Banglamphu is a great neighbourhood to graze in. Vendor carts make a patchwork quilt of the district, allowing ample sightseeing for a roving stomach. Thanks to the backpackers, vegetarians will find more sympathetic options here than elsewhere in this meat-loving city. The restaurants are casual and often spare on ambience, leaving more flair for the food.

🍴 ANN'S SWEET *Sweets* $$
☎ 0 86889 1383; 138 Th Phra Athit; ⏱ 10am-7pm; 🚌 32, 33, 64, 82, 🛥 Tha Phra Athit

Ann, a native of Bangkok and a graduate of the Cordon Bleu

cooking program, makes some of the most authentic Western-style cakes and sweets you'll find anywhere in town – great for a sugar-fuelled temple stop.

🍴 ARAWY *Thai Vegetarian* $

152 Th Din So; 🕐 8am-8pm; 🚌 10, 12, 🚣 khlong taxi to Tha Phan Fah; ♿ 🚹 Ⓥ

Curry-in-a-hurry is the aim of this tiny and inconspicuous vegie spot. Arawy was one of the city's first vegetarian restaurants and it's still going strong, serving premade dishes such as pumpkin stir-fry and green curry.

🍴 CHOTE CHITR *Thai* $$

☎ 0 2221 4082; 146 Th Phraeng Phuton; 🕐 11am-9pm Mon-Sat; 🚌 68, 516

Antique family-owned restaurants adorn this old section of town where middle-class Thais eat the way their parents and grandparents did before them. Chote Chitr is famous for *mèe gròrp* (sweet-and-spicy crispy fried noodles) and *yam hŏoa ƀlee* (banana-flower salad). *New York Times* food reviewer RW Apple ate here and loved it. It's located off Th Tanao.

🍴 HEMLOCK *Thai* $$

☎ 0 2282 7507; 56 Th Phra Athit; 🕐 4pm-midnight; 🚌 32, 33, 64, 82, 🚣 Tha Phra Athit; Ⓥ

You've met this restaurant before – remember that cosy gem where you wooed countless dates? Hemlock is just such a creature, boasting a steady cast of artsy types and a menu that reads like old literature.

🍴 ISAN RESTAURANTS

Northeastern Thai $

Th Ratchadamnoen Nok; 🕐 11am-10pm; 🚌 70, 503, 509

When a match is on at nearby Ratchadamnoen Boxing Stadium, these restaurants are run off their feet serving plates of Isan staples such as *gài yâhng* (grilled chicken), *sôm-đam* (green papaya salad) and *kôw něeo* (sticky rice).

🍴 KRUA APSORN *Thai* $$

Th Din So; 🕐 10am-8pm; 🚌 2, 15, 44, 511, 🚣 khlong taxi to Tha Phan Fah

---

TOOLS OF THE TRADE

We'll let you in on a secret: chopsticks are not a universally Asian utensil. In fact, Thais only use chopsticks for certain dishes, mainly those imported from China, such as noodle soups. Ever practical, Thais use a spoon and a fork for most dishes but the roles of these familiar items are utterly foreign. Thais use the fork much like Westerners use a knife to push food onto the spoon, which is used a lot like a fork. Still with us? The spoon delivers the food, while the fork remains behind.

A barbecue vendor prepares grilled delicacies before the crowds descend

GREG ELMS / LONELY PLANET IMAGES ©

This homey dining room has served members of the Thai royal family and, back in 2006, was recognised as Bangkok's Best Restaurant by the *Bangkok Post*. Must-eat dishes include mussels fried with fresh herbs, the decadent crab fried in yellow chilli oil and the tortilla Española–like crab omelette.

🍴 POJ SPA KAR *Thai* $
☎ 0 2222 2686; 443 Th Tanao; ⏱ 11am-9pm; 🚌 58, 516
This is reputedly Bangkok's oldest restaurant and continues to maintain recipes handed down from a former palace chef. The English-language menu could

---

DAY OFF

Fans of street food be forewarned that all of Bangkok's stalls close on Monday for compulsory street cleaning (the results of which are not entirely evident come Tuesday morning). If you happen to be in the city on this day, take advantage of the lull to visit one of the city's upscale hotel restaurants, which virtually never close.

In the mood for love at a streetside neighbourhood restaurant

GREG ELMS / LONELY PLANET IMAGES ©

use a grammar lesson, but good starting points include the unique lemon-grass omelette or the 'salad' of grilled pork and fresh herbs.

RICKY'S COFFEESHOP
International $$

☎ 0 2629 0509; 18 Th Phra Athit;
🕐 8am-11pm; 🚌 32, 33, 64, 82,
⚓ Tha Phra Athit; Ⓥ

A beautiful cafe decorated like an old Chinese teashop, decked out with old fans and cigarette-poster-girl prints. And it knows its road-warrior market well, serving the best filled baguettes in Banglamphu.

ROTI-MATABA *Thai-Muslim* $

☎ 0 2282 2119; 136 Th Phra Athit;
🕐 9.30am-9.30pm Tue-Sun; 🚌 32, 33,
64, 82, ⚓ Tha Phra Athit

Don't visit Banglamphu without stopping by Roti-Mataba. The rhythms of the roti makers as they slap and flip the Indian-style flatbread on the hotplate will draw you in. But spooning chicken korma or Thai/Muslim-style curries onto bites of crunchy roti will make your taste buds respect you.

SHOSHANA *Israeli* $

sub-soi off Th Chakraphong; 🕐 10am-
midnight; 🚌 32, 516, ⚓ Tha Phra
Athit; Ⓥ

Down an alley off Th Chakra-phong, Shoshana's is a favourite of cuisine-cruising travellers. The felafel-and-hummus plates are suitable gut bombs, but don't overlook the tasty baba ganoush.

THIP SAMAI *Thai* $
☎ 0 2221 6280; www.thipsamai.com; 313 Th Mahachai; ⏰ 5.30pm-2am; 🚌 8, 37, 47, ⚓ khlong taxi to Tha Phan Fah; ♿ ♨

The country's most common street food, *pàt tai* (thin rice noodles with tofu, vegetables, egg and peanuts), still retains its venerable footpath setting but it has been elevated (flavour-wise) to notoriety here at Thip Samai. Wrapped in a delicate egg crepe, the special noodles are spiked with prime shrimp and achieve the perfect texture. It must be seriously good if Thais are willing to pay this much (up to 120B) for a plate of noodles.

▼ DRINK
Th Khao San is hands-down one of the must-see watering holes in the city. After sundown, the street becomes an open saloon brimming with VW vans selling hummingbird-syrup cocktails and sidewalk tables littered with beer bottles. There's also a de facto human parade: exuber-ant backpackers, rebellious Thai youths and even a few curious yuppie Thais. The party snakes through to Th Rambuttri and Soi Ram Buttri, on either side of Th Chakraphong.

▼ AD HERE THE 13TH *Bar*
13 Th Samsen; ⏰ 5pm-midnight; 🚌 32, 516, ⚓ Tha Phra Athit

The best little dive bar in Thailand, Ad Here the 13th is a homey meet-ing place in which to have too many late nights and countless suds and cigs. The house band melts the night and the regulars' hearts with smoking blues tunes and rocking classics. Live music from 10pm.

▼ CENTER KHAO SAN *Bar*
☎ 0 2666 9999; Th Khao San; ⏰ 24hr; 🚌 32, 516, ⚓ Tha Phra Athit

STREET TROUBADORS
Th Khao San's next-door neighbour, Th Rambuttri, is palpably more chilled and significantly more sophisticated, as evidenced by the abundance of open-air pubs featuring live music, such as **Molly Bar** (☎ 0 2629 4074; 108 Th Rambuttri; ⏰ 8pm-1am; 🚌 32, 516, ⚓ Tha Phra Athit), **Suksabai** (☎ 0 2629 0298; 96 Th Rambuttri; ⏰ 24hr; 🚌 32, 516, ⚓ Tha Phra Athit) and **Barlamphu** (☎ 0 2282 2149; Th Rambuttri; ⏰ 11am-2am; 🚌 32, 516, ⚓ Tha Phra Athit).

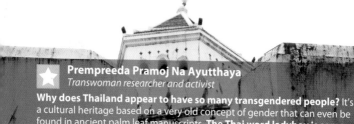

Prempreeda Pramoj Na Ayutthaya
Transwoman researcher and activist

Why does Thailand appear to have so many transgendered people? It's a cultural heritage based on a very old concept of gender that can even be found in ancient palm leaf manuscripts. **The Thai word ladyboy is sometimes used in English to refer to transgenders. How do you prefer to be called?** I prefer [the Thai word] *gà·teui* because it goes back to an indigenou Thai belief that sex isn't binary. The words ladyboy and shemale are often used to sell sex and can stigmatise transgenders. **To outsiders, Thailand appears very open to homosexuals and transgenders – is this really the case?** In everyday life, transgenders can live freely, but on a policy level we still face many difficulties. **What do you hope to achieve as an activist?** I'm working to change the laws and policies so that homosexuals and transgenders can feel more comfortable in Thailand.

As the name suggests, this centrally located, open-air pub is the best place for a front-row view of the human parade that is Th Khao San. An upstairs bar hosts late-night bands.

☿ HIPPIE DE BAR *Bar*
☎ 0 2629 3508; 46 Th Khao San;
⏱ 6pm-2am; 🚍 32, 516; ⛴ Tha Phra Athit

Popular with the locals, Hippie combines food, pool tables and one of the few playlists on Th Khao San that doesn't revolve around Jack Johnson or Bob Marley.

☿ PHRANAKORN BAR *Bar*
☎ 0 2282 7507; 58/2 Soi Damnoen Klang Tai; ⏱ 6pm-midnight; 🚍 2, 15, 44, 511, ⛴ khlong taxi to Tha Phan Fah

Phranakorn Bar is just steps away from Th Khao San but worlds removed. Students and arty types make this a home away from hovel with modest gallery exhibits, but the real draw here is a rooftop terrace for beholding the old district's majesty.

☿ ROLLING BAR *Bar*
Th Prachathipatai; ⏱ 6pm-midnight;
🚍 68, 516, ⛴ Tha Phra Athit

An escape from hectic Th Khao San is a good enough excuse to come to this quiet canal-side boozer. Tasty bar snacks and live music are reasons to stay.

★ PLAY

▦ BRICK BAR *Live Music*
☎ 0 2629 4477; basement, Buddy Lodge, 265 Th Khao San; ⏱ 7pm-2am;
🚍 32, 516, ⛴ Tha Phra Athit

This cavelike pub hosts a revolving line-up of live Thai music for an almost exclusively local crowd. If you're looking for something a bit more familiar, come at midnight and lose it to Teddy Ska, one of the most energetic live acts in town.

▦ RATCHADAMNOEN BOXING STADIUM *Muay Thai*
☎ 0 2281 4205; Th Ratchadamnoen Nok;
🚍 70, 503, 509

Muay thai fights are held at this bare-bones stadium four times a week: Monday, Wednesday, Thursday and Sunday at 6.30pm. Tickets cost 1000/1500/2000B (3rd class/2nd class/ringside). The stadium doesn't usually fill up until the main event around 8pm.

>THEWET & DUSIT

Rama V (King Chulalongkorn; r 1868–1910) returned from his grand tour of Europe with a building itch. He wanted his kingdom to reflect the regal flair he had witnessed in Europe. And so a new royal district was constructed in the area of Dusit, which was once a fruit orchard. As a result, the roads in Dusit are boulevards instead of converted canals and Rama V's new palace is fanciful and Victorian. But the unprecedented planning that went into creating Dusit left it uncharacteristically sterile for cramped and hyperactive Bangkok. The monuments to modern Thailand may look lovely from a car window; however, the broad footpaths are empty of street life, drawing more attention to the tropical heat than smart urban planning. After visiting Dusit Palace Park, the former royal residence, hop in a cab or túk-túk over to the riverside section of the district, referred to as Thewet, for an elixir of Bangkok village life, complete with markets, kids playing badminton and novice monks feeding the fish at the Thewet ferry pier.

THEWET & DUSIT

SEE

ABHISEK DUSIT THRONE HALL

☎ 0 2628 6300; Dusit Palace Park, Th Ratchawithi; ticket for all Dusit Palace Park sights 100/50B, free with Grand Palace ticket; ☼ 9.30am-4pm; 🚌 18, 28, 515; ♿

This Moorish-inspired building displays traditional Thai handicrafts such as silverware, blocks of teak carved into florid detail and geometrically patterned bamboo baskets. All the pieces have been created by members of the (deep breath) Foundation for the Promotion of Supplementary Occupations and Related Techniques (also known as Support), which has been set up to keep traditional skills alive and is sponsored by Queen Sirikit.

ANANTA SAMAKHOM THRONE HALL

☎ 0 2283 9411; www.artsofthekingdom .com; Th U Thong Nai; admission 150B; ☼ 10am-6pm Tue-Sun; 🚌 18, 28, 515

Adjacent to Dusit Palace Park, this imposing Italian-designed building was built as a royal reception hall during the reign of Rama V, but wasn't completed until 1915, five years after his death. Today the building houses an exhibit called Arts of the Kingdom, which, like the nearby Abhisek Dusit Throne Hall, displays the products of Queen Sirikit's Support foundation.

ANCIENT CLOTH MUSEUM

☎ 0 2628 6300; Dusit Palace Park, Th Ratchawithi; ticket for all Dusit Palace Park sights 100/50B, free with Grand Palace ticket; ☼ 9.30am-4pm; 🚌 18, 28, 515; ♿

Moorish design and Thai handicrafts are found at Abhisek Dusit Throne Hall   ANDERS BLOMQVIST / LONELY PLANET IMAGES ©

If you're interested in fashion, you should enjoy a poke around this museum, with its well-annotated collection of cloth, with accompanying information and exhibits on the weaving styles of the various Thai ethnic groups.

CHITLADA PALACE
cnr Th Ratchawithi & Th Phra Ram V; 18, 28, 515

The current royal family's residence, Chitlada Palace is also a royally funded agriculture centre demonstrating the reigning king's commitment to the progress of the country's major industry. The palace is not open to the public and it's pretty difficult to see from the outside, but you can spot rice paddies and animal pastures – smack in the middle of Bangkok – through the perimeter fence.

DUSIT PALACE PARK
0 2628 6300; bounded by Th Ratchawithi, Th U Thong Nai & Th Ratchasima; ticket for all Dusit Palace Park sights 100/50B, free with Grand Palace ticket; 9.30am-4pm; 18, 28, 515;

The oh-so-dainty Dusit Palace Park is the Thai monarchy's nod to the Victorian era. It contains Vimanmek Palace, the world's largest teak mansion, pleasant manicured grounds, the Ancient Cloth Museum and Royal Thai Elephant

Museum. For more information, see p22.

DUSIT ZOO
0 2281 2000; Th Phra Ram V; admission 100/50B; 8am-6pm; 18, 28, 515;

It would be easy to spend a day here. The peaceful grounds of this zoo, which once hosted the royal botanical garden, have a plethora of eateries as well as a playground and a big lake for paddle boating. The animal-housing areas are not the most modern or inviting. Located between Th Ratchawithi and Th Sri Ayuthaya.

ROYAL THAI ELEPHANT MUSEUM
0 2628 6300; Dusit Palace Park, Th Ratchawithi; ticket for all Dusit Palace Park sights 100/50B, free with Grand Palace ticket; 9.30am-4pm; 18, 28, 515;

Thais believe that albinism is auspicious, so all white elephants are considered royal property (Rama IX keeps one at his palace). Dusit Palace had two stables for keeping white elephants and this museum remembers these lucky creatures with displays explaining the ranks of elephants and their important role in Thai society.

RICHARD I'ANSON / LONELY PLANET IMAGES ©

Learn about the history of some unforgettable creatures at the Royal Thai Elephant Museum (p67)

THEWET FLOWER MARKET

Th Krung Kasem; 10am-6pm; 32, 516, Tha Thewet

Hardly a practical shopping option, this open-air market, located off Th Samsen, is more for windowless window-shopping than actual purchases. You'll discover from the selection that Bangkokians are avid container gardeners and can grow orchids and other exotic plants with minimal care.

VIMANMEK PALACE

0 2628 6300; Dusit Palace Park, Th Ratchawithi; ticket for all Dusit Palace Park sights 100/50B, free with Grand Palace ticket; 9.30am-4pm; 18, 28, 515;

This teak mansion was originally located on an island in the Gulf of Thailand, but was dismantled and reassembled, reputedly without nails, in 1901. Rama V took a three-storey octagonal apartment for himself and decorated his new home like the grand Victorian palaces he had seen in Europe. Women lived in a special green-coloured wing (the only men allowed inside were Rama V, a monk, a doctor and small boys). Viewing of the mansion is by guided tour only; tours run every 30 minutes from 9.45am to 3.15pm.

◎ WAT BENCHAMABOPHIT

cnr Th Sri Ayuthaya & Th Phra Ram V; admission 20B; ⏱ 8am-6pm; 🚌 72, 503; ♿

Buddha-image buffs find Wat Benchamabophit fascinating. Known as the 'Marble Temple' (it's made of white Carrara marble), it has a collection of 53 Buddha images representing different figures and styles from Thailand and other Buddhist countries. It was built during Rama V's reign; the temple's central Buddha image contains his ashes, and its cruciform *bòht* (central chapel) is a pure example of contemporary wat architecture.

🛍 SHOP

🛍 CHITLADA SHOP *Handicrafts*

☎ 0 2282 8435; Chitlada Palace, Th Ratchawithi; ⏱ 9.30am-3.30pm; 🚌 18, 28, 515; ♿

This is probably as close as you'll get to the royal family, so remember to dress respectfully (women must wear long skirts and closed shoes to gain entrance, men a shirt with collar). Located at the palace, this is an outlet of the nonprofit Support organisation, which promotes traditional craft-making skills.

RAINY-DAY TAXI

It never fails: when you need to get across town, the skies will unleash a monsoon storm. Bangkok's already crippled road transport starts to drown and cab drivers hold the coveted life-savers. Taxi drivers make their money with the flag fall, not with distance and definitely not from sitting in traffic. When the rains bring an increase of customers, the cabbies become picky, taking people who need a quick ride and turning down people who need more of a commitment. Don't take a stern headshake personally, it's only business in Bangkok.

🍴 EAT

🍴 KALOANG HOME KITCHEN

Thai $$

☎ 0 2668 8788; off Th Sri Ayuthaya; ⏱ 11am-11pm; 🚌 32, 516, ⚓ Tha Thewet

Don't be alarmed by the peeling paint and the dilapidated deck; Kaloang Home Kitchen certainly isn't. The laid-back atmosphere and seafood-heavy menu will quickly dispel any concerns about sinking into the Mae Nam Chao Phraya, and a beer and the breeze will temporarily erase any scarring memories of Bangkok traffic.

>CHINATOWN & PHAHURAT

Bangkok owes much of its urban identity to the labourers who left the Teochew region of China in the late 1700s in the hopes of finding their fortune in Siam. Many built mercantile empires in this riverside area from a few scraps of entrepreneurial brawn. Although many of the descendants have graduated into the elite strata of Bangkok society, Chinatown still retains its distinctive tie to the homeland with undiluted commerce. Shark-fin restaurants, gold and jade shops and huge neon signs in Chinese characters line Th Yaowarat, the district's main street. In the shadowy alleys, goods are unloaded by hand from crumbling warehouses and machine-repair shops stain the footpaths with motor oil.

To see Chinatown in business, come during the daylight to explore the various markets. But to savour Chinatown, come in the evenings when the streets off Th Yaowarat become nightly food markets.

Around the intersection of Th Phahurat and Th Chakraphet is a small but thriving Indian district, generally called Phahurat or Little India. Cramped storefronts are dominated by gem traders and fabric merchants.

For more information on this area, see p16.

CHINATOWN & PHAHURAT

🔵 SEE
Gurwara Siri Guru Singh
  Sabha Temple 1 B2
Nakhon Kasem 2 C2
Phra Buddha Maha
  Suwanna Patimakorn
  Exhibition ....(see 5)
Trok
  Itsaranuphap 3 D3
Wat Mangkon
  Kamalawat 4 D2
Wat Traimit 5 E3

Yaowarat Chinatown
  Heritage Center ....(see 5)

🔴 SHOP
Pak Khlong Market 6 A2
Phahurat Market 7 B2
Sampeng Lane Market ...8 C2

🍴 EAT
Jek Puy 9 D2
Mangkorn Khao 10 D3

Nay Mong 11 E2
Old Siam Plaza Food
  Centre 12 B2
Royal India 13 B2
Seafood Stalls 14 E3

⭐ PLAY
Chalermkrung Royal
  Theatre 15 B1

WORTH THE TRIP

Chinatown is organised like an ancient guild system – merchants of a feather flock together. Here's a guide to the streets and their mercantile persuasions.

> Th Charoen Krung: Chinatown's primary thoroughfare begins at the intersection of Th Mahachai with a collection of old record stores. Nearby Talat Khlong Ong Ang sells used, disused and unused electronic gadgets. Nakhon Kasem is the reformed 'thieves market' now stocking gadgets for portable food prep. Further east, Talat Khlong Thom is a hardware centre. West of Th Ratchawong, the stores cater to the afterlife and the passing of life.

> Th Yaowarat: this is Bangkok's gold street, the biggest trading centre of the precious metal in the country. Near the intersection of Th Ratchawong, stores shift to souvenirs for Chinese and Singaporean tourists. Tucked between the knick-knacks are a few apothecaries that smell like wood bark and ancient secrets.

> Th Mittraphan: signmakers branch off Wong Wian 22 Karakada; Thai and roman letters are typically cut out by a hand-guided lathe placed prominently beside the pavement.

> Th Santiphap: car parts and other automotive gear make this the place for kicking tyres.

💿 SEE

Chinatown is all about temples and markets – both of which are spectacles of busy bodies and cramped labyrinths.

🔵 GURWARA SIRI GURU SINGH SABHA TEMPLE

cnr Th Chakraphet & Th Phahurat; donations accepted; 🕑 9am-5pm; 🚌 82, 169, 507, 🚤 Tha Saphan Phut; ♿

This sleek and modern Sikh temple (it's kitted out with elevators and marble throughout) is devoted to Guru Granth Sahib, the Sikh holy scripture. You'll find the temple down a little alleyway off Th Chakraphet.

🔵 NAKHON KASEM

cnr Th Yaowarat & Th Chakrawat; 🕑 8am-8pm; 🚇 Hua Lamphong & access by taxi, 🚌 73, 159, 507, 🚤 Tha Ratchawong

Cooking equipment, spare electronic parts, and other bits you didn't know could be resold are on hand at this open-air market. During looser times, this was known as the 'thieves market', selling the fruits of the five-finger discount.

🔵 TROK ITSARANUPHAP (TALAT MAI)

Trok Itsaranuphap; 🕑 6am-6pm; 🚇 Hua Lamphong & access by taxi, 🚌 73, 159, 507, 🚤 Tha Ratchawong

Nudge your way deep into one of Chinatown's famous capillaries, where vendors sell dried goods, half-alive filleted fish and vats of unidentifiable pickled things. The *soi*'s (lane's) poetic finale is lined with stalls selling elaborate funeral offerings and 'passports to heaven' that include paper houses and cars to take loved ones into the next life. You'll find all the action between Sampeng Lane (Soi Wanit 1) and Th Yommarat Sukhum.

WAT MANGKON KAMALAWAT

Th Charoen Krung; donations accepted; 9am-6pm; Hua Lamphong & access by taxi, 73, 159, 507, Tha Ratchawong;

This Chinese temple is a labyrinth of vestibules. The gods of fortune in one of the first chambers is the most popular. Outside the temple, vendors sell heavenly food (oranges and steamed buns shaped like lotus flowers), purchased as offerings.

Heavenly pursuits at Wat Mangkon Kamalawat

WAT TRAIMIT

☎ 0 2623 1283; Th Traimit & Th Phra
Ram IV; admission 40B; ⏰ 8am-5pm
Tue-Sun; ◎ Hua Lamphong; ♿

The Temple of the Golden Buddha
sees a lot of visitors for one very
big reason: the world's largest
golden Buddha (5.5 tonnes and 3m
tall). A recent renovation has seen
the Golden Buddha relocated to a
four-storey marble structure that
towers over Chinatown. The 2nd
floor of the building is home to the
**Phra Buddha Maha Suwanna Patimakorn
Exhibition** (admission 100B; ⏰ 8am-5pm
Tue-Sun), which has exhibits on how
the statue was made, discovered
and came to arrive at its current
home. The 3rd floor is home to the
Yaowarat Chinatown Heritage Center
(admission 100B; ⏰ 8am-5pm Tue-Sun),
a small but engaging museum with
multimedia exhibits on the history
of Bangkok's Chinatown and its
residents.

🛍 SHOP
PAK KHLONG MARKET
Market

Th Chakkaphet; ⏰ 24hr; 🚌 3, 53, 83,
🚣 Tha Saphan Phut

Get up early or stay out late to
catch this 24-hour market, where
the city stocks up on orchids, lilies
and other tropical flowers. Pak
Khlong is also one of Bangkok's
fresh fruit and vegie markets.

GREG ELMS / LONELY PLANET IMAGES ©
Weird and wonderful knick-knacks keep buyers and vendors amused at Sampeng Lane Market

PHAHURAT MARKET *Market*

cnr Th Phahurat & Th Chakraphet; 10am-9pm; 🚌 82, 169, 507, 🛥 Tha Saphan Phut

A confusing warren of shops and narrow lanes makes up Little India's cloth and clothing market. You'll find saris, faux fur, bolts of fabric, rowdy prints, Thai dance costumes and a heck of a lot of kids' stuff (pyjamas, jumpers, bibs). But you might not find your way out.

SAMPENG LANE MARKET
Market

Sampeng Lane; 10am-10pm; 🚇 Hua Lamphong & access by taxi, 🚌 73, 159, 507, 🛥 Tha Ratchawong

You can get anything you want in Sampeng Lane (also known as Soi Wanit 1) as long as you appreciate the concept of economies of scale. Sandals? Take a 12-pack. Inflatable Superman? They've got five for 400B. If you look hard, you'll find some shopfronts selling tea and tobacco, just like in the old days.

EAT

When you say 'Chinatown', Bangkokians reflexively start slurping noodles. The neighbouring district of Phahurat (or Little India) dishes up curries and samosas.

STREET-EATS HEAVEN

For some of the tastiest of what Chinatown has to offer in one convenient location, head directly to the busy intersection of Th Yaowarat and Soi 11. There you'll find too many street vendors to list here, hocking everything from *pàt tai* (rice noodles with tofu, vegetables, egg and peanuts) to *gǒo·ay jáp nám sǎi*, a thick, intensely peppery broth containing noodles and pork offal. Remember to come in the evening and note that most street stalls are closed on Monday.

JEK PUY *Thai-Chinese* $

☎ 0 81850 9960; cnr Th Mangkon & Th Charoen Krung; 6-9pm Tue-Sun; 🚇 Hua Lamphong & access by taxi, 🚌 73, 159, 507, 🛥 Tha Ratchawong

Inconspicuous to the point of being invisible, this lauded curry stall proves Bangkokians' dedication to food over setting. Here's the catch: Jek Puy has no tables. Instead, diners sit on plastic stools in the middle of the sidewalk braving heat, noise and even rain in the wet season. All for a thick and flavourful bowl of *gaang gà·rèe*, a Chinese-style curry.

MANGKORN KHAO *Chinese* $

cnr Th Yaowarat & Th Yaowaphanit; 6-10pm Tue-Sun; 🚇 Hua Lamphong & access by taxi, 🚌 73, 159, 507, 🛥 Tha Ratchawong

Mangkorn Khao (White Dragon) is a respected vendor of *bà·mèe*

Nonstop Pak Khlong Market (p74) brims with fresh produce

AUSTIN BUSH / LONELY PLANET IMAGES ©

(Chinese-style wheat noodles) and delicious wontons. Top your bowl with the stall's baconlike barbecued pork or fresh crab.

NAY MONG *Thai-Chinese* $
☎ 0 2623 1890; 539 Th Phlap Phla Chai; ⏱ 6-11pm Tue-Sun; 🚇 Hua Lamphong & access by taxi, 🚌 73, 159, 507, ⛴ Tha Ratchawong

This tiny, family-run restaurant is renowned for its delicious *hŏy tôrt* (mussels or oysters fried with egg and a crispy-sticky batter). It also does a mean fried rice with crab.

OLD SIAM PLAZA FOOD CENTRE *Thai Sweets* $
ground fl, Old Siam Plaza, cnr Th Phahurat & Th Triphet; ⏱ 9am-6.30pm; 🚌 82, 169, 507, ⛴ Tha Saphan Phut; ♿ ♿

Beans, rice, tapioca, corn – Thais can turn seemingly savoury ingredients into extraordinarily sweet desserts. Peruse these transformations: *lôok chúp* (miniature fruits made of beans) and *kà·nŏm bêuang* (taco-shaped pancakes filled with shredded coconut and golden threads of sweetened egg yolk).

🍴 ROYAL INDIA *North Indian* $$
☎ 0 2221 6565; 392/1 Th Chakraphet; ⏲ 10am-10pm; 🚌 82, 169, 507, ⚓ Tha Saphan Phut; ♿ Ⓥ

You are unsure as you go down the dark laneway and open an unmarked door. Inside, tables of men are deep in discussion while a voluptuously moustached Indian man flogs golf clubs on cable TV. You soon discover that the food is incredible and the dhal indescribably delicious. Mission accomplished.

🍴 SEAFOOD STALLS
Chinese Seafood $$
cnr Th Yaowarat & Th Phadungdao; ⏲ 6-10pm Tue-Sun; Ⓔ Hua Lamphong & access by taxi, 🚌 73, 159, 507, ⚓ Tha Ratchawong

After the sun goes, this street sprouts outdoor barbecues, iced seafood trays and footpath seating. People serving food dash every which way, cars plough through narrow streets, and before you know it you're tearing into a plate of grilled prawns like a starved alley cat. Blaring Chinese pop music and limbless beggars will make your visit an extrasurreal experience.

⭐ PLAY

⭐ CHALERMKRUNG ROYAL THEATRE *Theatre*
☎ 0 2222 0434; www.salachalermkrung.com; cnr Th Charoen Krung & Th Triphet; tickets 800-1200B; ⏲ show 7.30-9pm; 🚌 3, 53, 83, ⚓ Tha Saphan Phut; ♿ ♿

This restored Thai Deco building, also known as Sala Chaloem Krung, hosts performances of *khon* (classical Thai dance-drama) every Thursday and Friday. Here *khon* is high-tech, with a flash audio system and computer-generated laser graphics. Dress respectfully (no shorts, sleeveless tops or sandals).

>SIAM SQUARE, PRATUNAM & PLOENCHIT

If sprawling Bangkok were to have a centre, this would be it. Yet no one calls it that. Instead, locals refer to the various municipal districts or major roads to keep their megacapital in bite-size pieces. The BTS train system, which sails along the backbone of modern Bangkok, has helped forge a sense of convergence and blocks of shopping malls have attached themselves to the stations like vacuum tubes leading directly into the stores. Amid this world of malls and office towers is an emerging fashion scene.

Not all of Bangkok has been erased by boxy shopping centres. Pratunam (Water Gate) retains a squatty village identity alongside Khlong Saen Saeb. At night the intersection of Th Phetchaburi and Th Ratchaprarop is a nucleus of outdoor dining, where families and friends are so absorbed by the meal that they ignore the capital's ever-present noise and pollution.

SIAM SQUARE, PRATUNAM & PLOENCHIT

SEE
Bangkok Art &
   Culture Centre **1** A2
Erawan Shrine **2** C2
Jim Thompson's House ..**3** A1
Lingam Shrine **4** E2
Siam Ocean World ....(see 20)

DO
Chic Club **5** B2
Spa 1930 ....**6** D3
Thann Sanctuary ......(see 19)

SHOP
Asia Books ....(see 20)
Central Chitlom **7** D2
Central World Plaza **8** C2
Digital Gateway ....(see 13)
Flynow ....(see 9)
Gaysorn Plaza **9** D2

It's Happened to
   Be a Closet **10** B2
Jaspal ....(see 18)
Jim Thompson ....(see 20)
Kinokuniya Books .....(see 20)
Madam Tussaud's .....(see 19)
Mae Fah Luang ....(see 19)
MBK **11** A2
Narai Phand **12** D2
New DJ Siam **13** B2
Pantip Plaza **14** C1
Pinky Tailors **15** E3
Pratunam Market **16** D1
Propaganda ....(see 19)
September **17** B2
Siam Center **18** B2
Siam Discovery
   Center **19** B2
Siam Paragon **20** B2
Siam Square **21** B2
Uthai's Gems **22** E4

EAT
Coca Suki **23** B2
Crystal Jade La Mian
   Xiao Long Bao **24** D2
Gourmet Paradise ......(see 20)
MBK Food Court ....(see 11)
Sra Bua **25** B1

DRINK
Ad Makers **26** E3
Café Trio **27** D3
Coco Walk **28** B1
Diplomat Bar **29** E4
Hyde & Seek ....(see 26)

PLAY
Calypso Cabaret **30** B1
Krung Sri IMAX ....(see 20)
Lido **31** B2
Scala **32** B2
SF Strike Bowl ....(see 11)

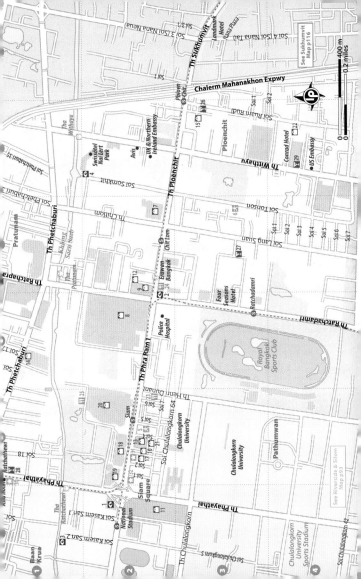

◉ SEE

◉ BANGKOK ART & CULTURE CENTRE

☎ 0 2214 6630; www.bacc.or.th; cnr Th Phayathai & Th Phra Ram I; admission free; ⏰ 10am-9pm Tue-Sun; 🚇 National Stadium; ♿

This immense, state-run complex combines art, performance and commerce in a multistorey building smack-dab in the centre of Bangkok. Go to the website to see what's on display.

◉ ERAWAN SHRINE

cnr Th Ploenchit & Th Ratchadamri; admission free; ⏰ 6am-11pm; 🚇 Chit Lom; ♿

ACCIDENT OR FOUL PLAY?

Jim Thompson's appreciation of Thai arts and crafts built a museum-worthy homestead as well as a successful silk business. But the cultural entrepreneur disappeared from his comfortable life under mysterious circumstances while visiting the Cameron Highlands, Malaysia, in 1967. Some muse that Jim Thompson, a former CIA agent, was snatched by communist spies, while others swear he met his maker between the fangs of a man-eating tiger. Much less fascinating, but far more likely, is that he was run over by a Malaysian truck driver.

In BKK commerce and religion are not mutually exclusive. This Brahman shrine was built after accidents delayed construction of the first Erawan Hotel. News of the shrine's protective powers spread and merit makers now stream into the courtyard with their own petitions.

◉ JIM THOMPSON'S HOUSE

☎ 0 2216 7368; www.jimthompson house.com; Soi Kasem San 2, Th Phra Ram I; admission 100/50B; ⏰ 9am-5pm, compulsory tours in English & French every 20min; 🚇 National Stadium

An American expat living in Bangkok assembled this collection of Thai art and architecture that visitors can appreciate on daily tours. The guides are professional and knowledgeable about the former resident and Thai traditions. For more information, see p25.

◉ LINGAM SHRINE

Nai Lert Park, Th Witthayu; admission free; ⏰ 24hr; 🚇 Chit Lom, 🚤 khlong taxi to Tha Withayu; ♿

This little shrine at the back of Swissôtel Nai Lert Park was built for the spirit of a nearby tree. But soon word spread that the shrine had fertility powers and a small forest of wooden phalluses sprung up, creating one of Bangkok's bawdiest shrines.

Lovingly selected art amid a luscious setting at Jim Thompson's House

MICK ELMORE / LONELY PLANET IMAGES ©

SIAM OCEAN WORLD

☎ 0 2687 2000; www.siamoceanworld.
co.th; basement, Siam Paragon, Th Phra
Ram I; tickets 900/700B; 🕒 10am-9pm;
🚇 Siam; ♿

Take the plunge into the underwater world of this massive
aquarium. The little ones can visit
the ocean depths in the glass-
enclosed Deep Reef zone or view
the daily feedings of penguins and
sharks (which aren't invited to the
same table).

🏃 DO

🧖 SPA 1930 *Spa*

☎ 0 2254 8606; www.spa1930.com;
42 Soi Tonson; treatments from 1000B,
packages from 3800B; 🕒 9.30am-
9.30pm; 🚇 Chit Lom; ♿

Discreet and sophisticated, Spa
1930 rescues relaxers from the
contrived spa ambience of New
Age music and ingredients you'd
rather see at a dinner party. The
menu is simple (face, body care
and body massage) and the scrubs
and massage oils are logical
players.

🧖 THANN SANCTUARY *Spa*

☎ 0 2658 0550; www.thann.info; 5th
fl, Siam Discovery Center, cnr Th Phayathai & Th Phra Ram I; 🕒 10am-9pm;
🚇 Siam; ♿

Get lured in for a sniff test of Thann's
all-natural, locally developed

SIAM SQUARE, PRATUNAM & PLOENCHIT

WORTH THE TRIP

Bangkok has many full-fledged attractions, but some of the most memorable sights are purely accidental. Here is a list of our favourites.

> Watching the cool kids hang out in **Siam Square** (p87)
> Joining the sweating-to-techno aerobics classes at **Lumphini** (p110) or **Santichaiprakan** (p53) parks
> Ogling the luxury cars in the 2nd-floor showroom at **Siam Paragon** (p86)
> Catching a commissioned dance at **Lak Meuang** (p42) or **Erawan Shrine** (p80)

body-care products. Lemon grass, lime, rosemary: all smell good enough to eat. Around the corner from the shop is the spa centre for post-shopping therapy. Also in Gaysorn Plaza (opposite).

🛍 SHOP

A visit to Bangkok's shopping malls is as important as the temple tours, and both invoke elements of the national character. Plus you can travel several kilometres in air-conditioning by weaving through the grove of shopping centres and the elevated walkways connecting to the BTS stations.

📖 ASIA BOOKS *Books*

☎ 0 2610 9609; 2nd fl, Siam Paragon, Th Phra Ram I; ☻ 10am-10pm; 🚇 Siam
One of the first English-language bookstores in Thailand, Asia Books continues to dominate the market with a wide selection of books as well as magazines. Also at Siam Discovery Center (p86) and the Emporium (p121).

🏬 CENTRAL CHITLOM

Shopping Centre

☎ 0 2793 7777; 1027 Th Ploenchit; ☻ 10am-10pm; 🚇 Chit Lom; 🛗
In this internationally educated department store, executive-strength credit cards cruise the escalators thumbing homewares, *fa·ràng*-sized (Westerner-sized) clothes and cosmetics.

🏬 CENTRAL WORLD PLAZA

Shopping Centre

☎ 0 2635 1111; www.centralworld. co.th; Th Ratchadamri & Th Phra Ram I; ☻ 10am-10pm; 🚇 Chit Lom, Siam; 🛗
Bangkok's hippest mall suffered greatly during the unrest of April 2010, but the vast majority of shops are again open and Zen department store was being rebuilt at research time. Highlights include outlets of all the local labels, with an extra-huge branch of the bookstore B2S, and you could spend an hour sniffing around the fragrances at Karmakamet

(2nd floor). An elevated walkway links Central World to the BTS and several other local megamalls.

FLYNOW *Fashion*
☎ 0 2656 1359; 2nd fl, Gaysorn Plaza, cnr Th Ploenchit & Th Ratchadamri; ⏰ 10am-9pm; 🚉 Chit Lom; ♿

This Bangkok-born label has flown its flowing, feminine designs all the way to London and back (having opened at London Fashion Week twice) and still lands effortlessly on the daily runways of Bangkok's fashion elite. Also in Siam Paragon (p86).

GAYSORN PLAZA
Shopping Centre
☎ 0 2656 1149; cnr Th Ploenchit & Th Ratchadamri; ⏰ 10am-10pm; 🚉 Chit Lom; ♿

This fashion palace accommodates all the haughty international designers (Gucci, Prada, Louis Vuitton et al) plus Thai high-flyers (Flynow and senada*), giving credibility to the city's self-endowed title, 'Fashion City'. Gaysorn's top floor is also one of Bangkok's best one-stop shopping destinations for high-end home decor, the highlights of which include the eclectic D&O Shop, the fragrant soaps at Thann and the Asian-influenced ceramics at Lamont.

JASPAL *Fashion*
☎ 0 2251 5918; 2nd fl, Siam Center, cnr Th Phayathai & Th Phra Ram I; ⏰ 10am-10pm; 🚉 Siam; ♿

With a finger on the pulse of Western trends and a constant eye on the international fash mags, Jaspal is a high-street label for guys and girls not born in the silver-spoon league. There's also a branch at the Emporium (p121).

JIM THOMPSON *Fashion*
Siam Paragon, Th Phra Ram I; ⏰ 10am-10pm; 🚉 Siam

Yet another mall-based outlet of the acclaimed Thai silk brand. Also on Th Surawong (p98) and at the Emporium (p121).

KINOKUNIYA BOOKS *Books*
☎ 0 2610 9500; 3rd fl, Siam Paragon, Th Phra Ram I; ⏰ 10am-10pm; 🚉 Siam; ♿

Bangkokians will have to adopt some diligent reading habits to support this huge bookstore

---

CALL ME LUCKY

Think telephone numbers are just a batch of digits associated with your phone? In Thailand, a lucky telephone number is the key to success. On the 4th floor of MBK, telephone numbers with auspicious combinations (nines are golden) are auctioned off like antique collections.

in Siam Paragon – the English-language options and magazines are virtually endless. Also at the Emporium (p121).

MAE FAH LUANG *Fashion*
☎ 0 2658 0424; www.doitung.org; 4th fl, Siam Discovery Center, cnr Th Phayathai & Th Phra Ram I; ⏱ 10am-10pm; 🚇 Siam; ♿

Another handwoven tradition, these cotton textiles are produced as part of HRH the late Princess Mother's program to transition northern Thailand villages away from opium production. Bolts of fabric are sold alongside ready-to-wear women's designs that update this ethnic-hippie fabric into new-millennium styles.

MBK *Shopping Centre*
Mah Boon Krong; ☎ 0 2620 9000; cnr Th Phra Ram I & Th Phayathai; ⏱ 10am-10pm; 🚇 National Stadium; ♿

Fast becoming Bangkok's most famous mall, MBK is a drier indoor version of the wet Asian market. You'll find lots of ordinary bargains as well as crowds of savvy shoppers. For more information, see p26.

NARAI PHAND *Handicrafts*
☎ 0 2656 0398; www.naraiphand.com; ground fl, President Tower, 973 Th Ploenchit; ⏱ 10am-8pm; 🚇 Chit Lom; ♿

As a not-for-profit enterprise for distributing villagers' handicrafts, Narai Phand has its heart in the right place, although it feels a bit like a souvenir factory. Regardless, the gaudy souvenirs are handy.

NEW DJ SIAM *Music*
☎ 0 22251 2513; 292/16 Siam Square, Soi 4; ⏱ 10am-7pm; 🚇 Siam; ♿

In the heart of teen-landia, this tiny store feeds the kiddies with the hottest overseas alt-options as well as all the Thai-bred indie groups.

ALL THAT GLITTERS
Ah, the gem scam. We all know of someone who's been duped but still the Land of Smiles keeps relieving us of untold sums. Let the warning bells ring when a friendly local and/or fellow national approaches you and casually asks you along to their friend's gem (and/or tailoring) shop or a one-day-only sale. The gem scam usually ends with you being talked into buying low-grade unset gems and posting them home, where you'll find out they're worth very little. Just remember that the gem trade is a long and established industry that doesn't need your help in circumventing import regulations. A deal too good to be true almost certainly is.

Go underwater without getting wet at Siam Ocean World (p81)

GREG ELMS / LONELY PLANET IMAGES ©

🏠 PANTIP PLAZA *Shopping Centre*

Th Phetchaburi; 🕙 10am-8pm;
🚈 Ratchathewi, 🚤 khlong taxi to Tha
Pratunam

For the time being Pantip is the Wild West of computer components. Discounted pirated software, fresh off the factory conveyor belts, is the primary draw, turning obedient citizens into reckless law-breakers. Hardware junkies work the floors for used parts to beef up ailing machines.

🏠 PINKY TAILORS *Tailor*

☎ 0 2253 6328; 888/40 Mahatun Plaza
Arcade, Th Ploenchit; 🕙 10am-7.30pm
Mon-Sat; 🚈 Phloen Chit

Custom-made suit jackets are Mr Pinky's speciality. He also has a quiet, no-hassle shop where you can touch all of the fabrics without stumbling over a sales associate. Behind the Mahatun Building.

🏠 PRATUNAM MARKET *Market*

cnr Th Phetchaburi & Th Ratchaprarop;
🕙 10am-9pm; 🚌 505, 511, 🚤 khlong
taxi to Tha Pratunam

The city's biggest wholesale clothing market, Pratunam is a tight warren of stalls trickling deep into the block. In addition to cheap T-shirts and jeans, luggage, bulk toiletries and souvenirs are also available.

🖾 PROPAGANDA *Homewares*

☎ 0 2664 8574; 4th fl, Siam Discovery Center, cnr Th Phayathai & Th Phra Ram I; ⏰ 10am-10pm; 🚇 Siam; ♿

If Propaganda is truly trying to live up to its name, then count us as officially indoctrinated. It's hard to resist the charms of this fun, stark-white shop with all sorts of functional design pieces created by Thai designers, such as Chaiyut Plypetch's lamps featuring the an-

---

THE ELECTRONICS MYTH

Somewhere in cyberspace or by word of mouth, folks got the crazy idea that Bangkok is a mecca for cheap electronics. Because we care, here is the truth: digital cameras, laptops and other new gadgets are going to cost you the same or more in Bangkok than back home. Where techies do win is in Bangkok's still untamed frontier for intellectual property. Despite pressures on Thai officials for IP enforcement, everyone's favourite contraband, pirated software and music, is outrageously cheap in the Land of Knock-Offs.

---

atomically cartoonish Mr P. There's another Propaganda branch at the Emporium (p121).

🖾 SIAM CENTER & SIAM DISCOVERY CENTER

Shopping Centre

☎ 0 2658 1000; cnr Th Phayathai & Th Phra Ram I; ⏰ 10am-10pm; 🚇 Siam; ♿

These sister centres fill in the budget range between proletariat MBK and luxe Siam Paragon. The Discovery Center has a little bit of everything, including an Asian-heavy branch of **Madam Tussaud's** (☎ 0 2658 0060; www.madametussauds. com/Bangkok/en; 6th fl; tickets 600-800B; ⏰ 10am-9pm), but mainly stylish home-furnishing stores. Follow the pouty, mobile-phone crowd to link with Siam Center, which has been rebranded for the younger set with more fashion (particularly local brands) and thumping techno.

🖾 SIAM PARAGON

Shopping Centre

☎ 0 2690 1000; www.siamparagon. co.th; Th Phra Ram I; ⏰ 10am-10pm; 🚇 Siam; ♿

A shopper could dive in and never resurface in this airport-sized mall dedicated mainly to a Milky Way of famous luxury brands. More popular is the lobby atrium, referred to by some Thais as their new park, and the basement-level Gourmet Paradise (p88). If you collect trivia, this is allegedly the biggest mall in Southeast Asia.

🖼 SIAM SQUARE *Shopping Centre*
Th Phra Ram I; ⏰ most stores 10am-9pm; 🚇 Siam

The closest Bangkok comes to a boutique district is the open-air shopping complex, near the intersection of Th Phayathai, known as Siam Square. This is ground-zero for youth fashion, wedged between MBK and Chulalongkorn University. Bottle-like **Digital Gateway** (btwn Soi 3 & Soi 4) is your destination if you need anything digital, while closet-sized boutiques line Soi 2, 3 and 4. Some recent winners include **September** (☎ 0 1815 8641; Soi 3, Siam Square) and **It's Happened to Be a Closet** (☎ 0 2985 9345; 266/3 Soi 3, Siam Square).

🖼 UTHAI'S GEMS *Jewellery*
☎ 0 2253 8582; 28/7 Soi Ruam Rudi; ⏰ 10am-6pm Mon-Sat; 🚇 Phloen Chit

Uthai's Gems showroom is in quiet Soi Ruam Rudi serving the discriminating embassy community. Nonhagglers appreciate his fixed prices and good service. Appointments recommended.

🍴 EAT
From mall munching to causes célèbres, Siam Square and nearby Th Ploenchit, Th Ratchadamri and Th Witthayu offer a full house of eating options.

GREG ELMS / LONELY PLANET IMAGES ©
Escalators to shopping heaven, Siam Paragon

🍴 COCA SUKI *Thai* $$
☎ 0 2251 6337; 416/3-8 Th Henri Dunant; ⏰ 11am-11pm; 🚇 Siam; 🚻 🧒 Ⓥ

Immensely popular among Thai families, the domestic version of *sukiyaki* takes the form of a bubbling hotpot of broth and a platter of raw ingredients to dip therein. Heat junkies be sure to request the tangy 'tom yam' broth. Although Coca is one of the oldest purveyors of the dish, the Siam Square branch reflects the brand's efforts to appear more modern.

VIP DINING

Although Thai meals appear very informal, there are many subtle gestures of honour and communal gestures extended to guests and elders. Most Thais will pick out the most delicious pieces of a whole fish and serve it to their guest (that typically means you) or make sure that you receive spoonfuls of dishes too far away to reach yourself. Also notice that the person closest to the drink bottles or the serving dish of rice becomes the de facto server, loading up everyone else before plunging in themselves. To show your appreciation for the meal, leave a little rice on your plate to signal satiation.

The communal spirit of a Thai meal is even more apparent when eating the kingdom's famous curries *(gaang)* and soups (such as *dôm yam gûng*). Both arrive at the table in a single bowl from which diners ladle for each other the contents into individual bowls and then spoon the edible bits onto rice. Not everything in a *dôm yam* can be eaten; if it is hard to chew, then you've discovered the Thai version of bay leaves. After sharing a Thai meal, our Western manners might seem a tad selfish.

🍴 CRYSTAL JADE LA MIAN XIAO LONG BAO *Chinese* $$

☎ 0 2250 7990; Urban Kitchen, basement, Erawan Bangkok, 494 Th Ploenchit; ⏰ 11am-10pm; 🚇 Chit Lom; ♿ 🚼 Ⓥ

The comically long moniker of this Singaporean franchise checks the restaurant's signature hand-pulled wheat noodles (*la mian*) and the famous Shanghai steamed dumplings (*xiao long bao*). The remainder of the menu is an edible map of China, spanning Peking duck to Hong Kong–style vegies. Prices are higher than the street noodle stall just around the corner, but you're paying for quality.

🍴 GOURMET PARADISE

Thai, International $$

☎ 0 2610 8000; ground fl, Siam Paragon, Th Phra Ram I; ⏰ 10am-9pm; 🚇 Siam; ♿ 🚼 Ⓥ

A whole floor is dedicated to food in Siam Paragon's ubermall universe. The feudal divisions of Thai society are in full evidence at weekends: aristocrats file into the branches of successful white-linen restaurants; the working class hustles through the food court with trays of noodles and stir-fries.

🍴 MBK FOOD COURT

Thai-Chinese $

6th fl, MBK, cnr Th Phra Ram I & Th Phayathai; ⏰ 10am-10pm; 🚇 National Stadium; ♿ 🚼 Ⓥ

It's a lot like having all your favourite street-food vendors in one place. There is no need to visit the noodle woman in one street, the fruit-juice man in another and then hike to find a stall for mango and sticky rice. Come early for the popular vegetarian stall.

SRA BUA *Thai* $$$

☎ 0 2162 9000; www.kempinskibangkok.com; ground fl, Siam Kempinski Hotel, 991/9 Th Rama I; 🕐 noon-3pm & 6-11pm Mon-Fri, 6-11pm Sat & Sun; 🚇 Siam; ♿ ♨

Helmed by a Thai and a Dane whose Copenhagen restaurant, Kiin Kiin, holds a Michelin star, Sra Bua takes a correspondingly international approach to Thai

---

FOOD WITHOUT THE FUMES

Shopping-centre food courts are usually examples of food abuse, but Bangkok's food courts retain the same dedication to flavours as their streetside brethren and without the noise or heat. All the shopping centres have one, but MBK's food court, Siam Paragon's Gourmet Paradise and Central Chitlom's FoodLoft are genre standouts. The process works like this: first you buy coupons or a debit card from a designated booth and use this intermediary currency to buy food. A refund for any unspent money is available on the day of purchase.

---

food – think frozen red curry with lobster.

🍸 DRINK

🍸 AD MAKERS *Bar*

☎ 0 2168 5158; ground fl, Athenee Residence, 65/1 Soi Ruam Rudi; 🕐 11am-2pm & 5pm-1am Mon-Fri, 5pm-1am Sat & Sun; 🚇 Phloen Chit

The most recent incarnation of this longstanding bar/restaurant – originally started up in 1985 by a group of ad executive buddies – draws in diners and partiers with tasty regional Thai eats and live tunes (from Tuesday to Saturday).

🍸 CAFÉ TRIO *Bar*

☎ 0 2252 6572; 36/11-12 Soi Lang Suan; 🕐 6pm-midnight Mon-Sat; 🚇 Chit Lom

Café Trio meets so few strangers that it is expected for you to introduce yourself upon arrival. Patti is the mistress of ceremonies and will make sure you drink more than you intended. Her subjects, a regular crowd of diplomats and professionals, are happy to toast her every whim.

🍸 COCO WALK *Bar*

87/70 Th Phayathai; 🕐 6pm-1am; 🚇 Ratchathewi

This covered compound is a smorgasbord of pubs, bars and live music popular with Thai university students. The Tube left its heart in London, and is heavy

89

Razzle-dazzle on stage at Calypso Cabaret   MICK ELMORE / LONELY PLANET IMAGES ©

on Britpop; Chilling House Café features Thai hits played by live acoustic guitar, and a few pool tables; and 69 sets the pace with cover bands playing Western rock staples and current hits.

 DIPLOMAT BAR *Bar*

☎ 0 2690 9999; ground fl, Conrad Hotel, 87 Th Witthayu; ⏰ 6pm-midnight; ⓧ Phloen Chit

Young sophisticates toast their fortune and looks at one of Bangkok's leading hotel bars. The bubbly and the grapey spirits are the tipples of choice while the diva-led lounge band serenades.

HYDE & SEEK *Bar*

☎ 0 2168 5152; ground fl, Athenee Residence, 65/1 Soi Ruam Rudi; ⏰ 11am-1am; ⓧ Phloen Chit

The tasty and comforting English-inspired bar snacks and meals have earned Hyde & Seek the right to call itself a 'gastro bar', but we reckon the real reasons to come are arguably Bangkok's most well-stocked bar and some of the city's best cocktails.

⭐ PLAY

When it is hot and steamy outside, Bangkok's plush cinemas are a welcome escape. Dozens of theatres screen movies in English, with

Thai subtitles; check the *Bangkok Post* or www.movieseer.com for session times. Tickets cost around 150B for basic seating and up to 600B for VIP. The royal anthem is played before every screening and patrons are expected to stand respectfully.

☆ CALYPSO CABARET
Transexual Cabaret

☎ 0 2653 3960; www.calypsocabaret.com; Asia Hotel, 296 Th Phayathai; tickets 1200B; ☼ shows 8.15pm & 9.45pm; 🚇 Ratchathewi

Watching men dressed as women perform tacky show tunes has, not surprisingly, become the latest 'must-do' fixture on the Bangkok tourist circuit. Calypso hosts choreographed stage shows featuring Broadway high kicks and lip-synched pop tunes by the most well-endowed dudes you'll find anywhere.

☆ KRUNG SRI IMAX *Cinema*

☎ 0 2515 5555; www.imaxthai.com; 5th fl, Siam Paragon, Th Phra Ram I; tickets 600/250B; 🚇 Siam; ♿ ♿

Be engulfed by the big-screen technology of IMAX at this huge modern theatre. Screenings range

---

WHICH WAY TO TOLLYWOOD?

If you've got your eye on the silver screen, Thailand is emerging as an art-movie darling. Bangkok's International Film Festival (www.bangkokfilm.org) screens Thai talent, as do art-house cinemas such as **Lido** (☎ 0 2252 6498; Siam Square, Th Phra Ram I; 🚇 Siam), **Scala** (☎ 0 2251 2861; Siam Square Soi 1, Th Phra Ram I; 🚇 Siam) and **House** (Map p134, F5; ☎ 0 2641 5177; www.houserama.com; UMG Building, RCA/Royal City Avenue, near Th Phetchaburi; 🚇 Phra Ram 9 & access by taxi).

---

from nature features of audience-hunting sharks to special-effects versions of Hollywood action flicks.

☆ SF STRIKE BOWL *Bowling*

☎ 0 2611 4555; 7th fl, MBK, cnr Th Phra Ram I & Th Phayathai; games from 30B; ☼ 10am-1am; 🚇 National Stadium; ♿

Thai teenagers crowd this psychedelically decorated bowling alley at all hours of the day and night. The cost varies, depending what time you play.

>RIVERSIDE & SILOM

Swollen ships dispensed exotic goods and explorers on the riverside docks that once defined Bangkok's early port. Remnants of this era are preserved along the little lanes that wind through abandoned warehouses and crumbling neoclassical palaces facing the river. The new kings of the river are the luxury riverside hotels that drink in the watery and romantic view. Tucked in between are Muslim and Indian communities that replaced the old European mercantile class.

As the modern era nudged out shipping, business migrated inland along Bangkok's financial district of Th Silom. During the week, the streets are packed with office workers en route to lunch stalls or business meetings while blind troubadours hope for spare bits of their lunch money. The crush of bodies makes Western cities look like sleepy

RIVERSIDE & SILOM

◉ SEE
Bangkok Folk Museum ..**1** C2
Holy Rosary Church **2** B1
Kathmandu Photo
   Gallery **3** D3
Queen Saovabha Memorial
   Institute Snake Farm ..**4** F1
San Jao Sien Khong **5** A1
Sri Mahariamman
   Temple **6** D3
Talat Noi **7** A1

🎎 DO
Fortune Tellers **8** E2
Healthland Spa &
   Massage **9** D3
Oriental Spa Thai Health
   & Beauty Centre **10** A3
Ruen-Nuad Massage
   Studio **11** F3
Silom Thai Cooking
   School **12** D3

🛍 SHOP
H Gallery **13** D3
House of Chao **14** D2
House of Gems **15** B3
Jim Thompson **16** F1
Lin Silvercraft **17** B3
Maison des Arts **18** B3
Old Maps & Prints ...(see 20)
Patpong Night Market ..**19** F2
River City **20** B1
Silom Village Trade
   Centre **21** D3
Soi Lalai Sap Market **22** E2
S.V. Jewelery **23** B3
Thai Home Industries ..**24** B3
Thavibu Gallery **25** C3

🍴 EAT
Foodie **26** E3
Indian Hut **27** C2
Kalpapruek Restaurant .**28** D3
Krua 'Aroy-Aroy' **29** D3
Le Normandie ......(see 41)
Mizu's Kitchen **30** F2

Naaz **31** C2
Nadimos **32** C3
Scoozi **33** E2
Soi 10 Food Centres **34** E2
Somboon Seafood **35** E2
Somtam Convent **36** F2
Taling Pling **37** D3
Wan Fah Cruises **38** B1
Yok Yor Marina &
   Restaurant **39** A2

🍸 DRINK
Balcony Bar **40** F2
Bamboo Bar ....(see 41)
Oriental Hotel's
   Author's Lounge **41** B3
Sirocco & Sky Bar **42** C3
Telephone **43** F2

⭐ PLAY
DJ Station **44** F2
G.O.D. **45** F2
Sala Rim Naam .....(see 41)
Tapas Room **46** F2

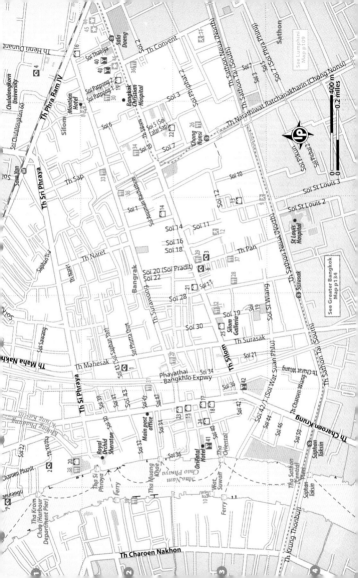

villages. Unless you've come with briefcase in tow, you'll meet Silom at night thanks to the infamous red-light district of Patpong, now a tamer skin circus and souvenir market.

SEE

Sightseeing is limited in these parts, but the lanes between the river and Th Charoen Krung are good candidates for wandering. Th Silom used to be the outskirts of the city, evidenced by the European and Chinese cemeteries around Soi 11.

BANGKOK FOLK MUSEUM
☎ 0 2233 7027; 273 Soi 43 (Soi Saphan Yao), Th Charoen Krung; admission free; 🕙 10am-4pm Wed-Sun; 🚌 75, 504, 🚢 Tha Oriental

Also known as the Bangkokian Museum, this family-run museum comprised of a compound of attractive wooden houses is a window into Bangkok life during the 1950s and '60s. Particularly interesting is the traditional Thai kitchen.

KATHMANDU PHOTO GALLERY
☎ 0 2234 6700; www.kathmandu-bkk. com; 87 Th Pan; 🕙 11am-7pm Tue-Sun; 🚇 Surasak

Manit Sriwanichpoom, one of Bangkok's leading photographers, has opened his own gallery in a refurbished Chinese-style shop-house. Rotating exhibits by friends and peers are featured in the up-stairs gallery, while the downstairs space is dedicated to the owner's portfolio.

QUEEN SAOVABHA MEMORIAL INSTITUTE SNAKE FARM
☎ 0 2252 0161; cnr Th Phra Ram IV & Th Henri Dunant; admission 200/50B; 🕙 9.30am-3.30pm Mon-Fri, to 1pm Sat & Sun, shows & milkings 11am & 2.30pm Mon-Fri, 11am Sat & Sun; 🚇 Sala Daeng, 🚇 Si Lom; ♿

This snake farm, one of only a few worldwide, was established in 1923 to breed snakes for antivenins. The snake shows are a nice sideline, where snake handlers educate visitors about snakes and freak them out by letting the baddest ones loose (don't fret, you're safe in the stands).

SRI MAHARIAMMAN TEMPLE
cnr Th Pan & Th Silom; donations accepted; 🕙 6am-8pm; 🚌 15, 504, 🚇 Surasak; ♿

Built by Tamil immigrants in the 1860s, this Hindu temple is a colourful place of worship in every sense of the word, from the multihued main temple to the

Korakot 'Nym' Punlopruksa
Storyteller

You do a lot of 'fixing' for foreign journalists and television programs. What is it about Bangkok that foreigners like most? Freedom, food and fun in everything. It's a place full of unexpected surprises. **If you were asked by a film crew to take them to the most photogenic part of Bangkok, where would you go?** Dawn at the flower market (Pak Khlong Market; p74). There's the beauty of the wet street reflecting the light, and the speed and colour of flowers and moving traffic. **What's the most underrated part of Bangkok?** Th Khao San. It's not only backpackers; there are lots of interesting places to eat and cosy live music bars. **What's your favourite part of Bangkok?** I like the old areas around Th Charoen Krung (Talat Noi; p96). It has a sense of community almost like a village: old noodle restaurants; shops selling umbrellas, incense and candles; the same orange juice squeezers and vendors on streets…

eclectic range of people of many faiths and ethnicities who come to make offerings. Thais call it Wat Khaek.

🌀 TALAT NOI
Th Phanurangsi; admission free;
🕐 9am-6pm; ⚓ Tha Si Phraya
Bordered by the river, Th Songwat, Th Charoen Krung and Th Yotha, this ancient neighbourhood is a fascinating jumble of tiny alleys, greasy machine shops and traditional architecture. Located below the River View Guest House, **San Jao Sien Khong** (admission by donation; 🕐 6am-6pm) is one of the city's oldest Chinese shrines and also one of the best areas to be during the annual Vegetarian Festival in October.

🏃 DO
Despite being home to Patpong's 'ping-pong' strip clubs, you can collect holiday moments that don't need censoring. Try out a Thai cooking class or massage therapy (the legitimate version).

🏃 FORTUNE TELLERS
Fortune Tellers
☎ 0 2234 8060; mezzanine level, Montien Hotel, Th Surawong; consultations 650B; 🕐 10am-4pm; ⚓ Sala Daeng, Ⓜ Si Lom; ♿
Thais regard fortune tellers as professional consultants whose

guidance is sought for picking auspicious dates to start businesses or marriages. In the most Thai of Thai hotels, space is devoted to this important business service, which includes two English speakers (a palmist and tarot-card reader).

🏃 HEALTHLAND SPA & MASSAGE *Spa, Massage*
☎ 0 2637 8883; www.healthlandspa. com; cnr Soi 12 & Th Sathon Neua; 2hr massage 450B; 🕐 9am-11pm; ⚓ Surasak; ♿
The name and the supersized setting might suggest massage factory, but Bangkok locals swear this is one of the best-value massages in the city. The massage component of this business started out as an add-on service to an organic grocery store in the Bangkok suburbs.

🏃 ORIENTAL SPA THAI HEALTH & BEAUTY CENTRE *Spa*
☎ 0 2659 9000; www.mandarinorien tal.com; Oriental Hotel, 48 Soi 40/Oriental, Th Charoen Krung; day packages from 2900B; 🕐 9am-10pm; ⚓ Saphan Taksin, 🚌 75, 504, ⚓ free shuttle boat from Tha Sathon; ♿
One of Bangkok's most private and intimate spas, the Oriental has 14 rooms in a classic setting. You won't find a lot of bells and whistles here, just the necessary

niceties. The most popular therapy offered is the jet-lag massage, which will help reset an obstinate body clock.

RUEN-NUAD MASSAGE STUDIO *Massage*

☎ 0 2632 2662; 42 Th Convent, Th Silom; massage per hr 350B; ☽ 10am-9pm; 🚇 Sala Daeng, ⊕ Si Lom

For a Goldilocks massage (not too hard, not too soft), Ruen-Nuad offers a tranquil spa-like setting but at parlour-shop prices.

✈ SILOM THAI COOKING SCHOOL *Cooking School*

☎ 0 84726 5669; www.bangkokthaicooking.com; 68 Soi 13, Th Silom; classes 1000B; ☽ 9am-1pm & 1.40-6pm; 🚇 Chong Nonsi

Run out of a private home, this is an introduction to both home cooking and ordinary Thai life. The setting is rustic (and not hyper-hygienic) and you chop shallots while sitting cross-legged on the floor, pound chillies into paste, and fry it all up in the pan. Includes a market tour and six dishes.

🛍 SHOP

The majority of Bangkok's antique stores congregate near their potential customers on Th Charoen Krung, near the riverside hotels.

RICHARD I'ANSON / LONELY PLANET IMAGES ©

Relax at Oriental Spa Thai Health & Beauty Centre

🖼 H GALLERY *Art*

☎ 0 81310 4428; www.hgallerybkk.com; Soi 12, Th Sathon Neua; ☽ 10am-6pm Wed-Sat; 🚇 Surasak

H is a conduit for aspiring abstract artists deemed worthy enough to percolate into its New York gallery. Open on Tuesday by appointment only.

🖼 HOUSE OF CHAO *Antiques*

☎ 0 2635 7188; 9/1 Th Decho; ☽ 9.30am-7pm; 🚇 Chong Nonsi, 🚌 15, 504; ♿

Dusty old antique shops littered with precious and not-so-precious junk are rare in Bangkok, but this spot is haphazardly filled with teak treasures from Thailand and Myanmar.

🏠 HOUSE OF GEMS *Antiques*
☎ 0 2234 6730; 1218 Th Charoen Krung; 🕐 8am-6pm Mon-Sat; 🚌 75, 504, 🚢 Tha Oriental

The name 'House of Gems' is an interesting sales pitch for a shop claiming to sell dinosaur droppings. If you look in the window, dry cross-sections will teach you the subtle difference between the 'gems' of a carnivorous dinosaur, compared to its herbivorous friends. Don't say we didn't tell you that there's nothing you can't buy in Bangkok.

🏠 JIM THOMPSON *Fashion*
☎ 0 2632 8100; www.jimthompson. com; 9 Th Surawong; 🕐 9am-9pm; 🚇 Sala Daeng, 🚇 Si Lom

As you'd expect of the company that resurrected the Thai silk industry, you get nothing but impeccable fabric here. You can buy silk by the metre (which can be tailored on-site), silk scarves and neckties and accessories (including tablecloths, throw pillows and napkins). Jim Thompson stores are also located at the Emporium (p121) and Siam Paragon (p86) shopping centres.

Journey through historic Siam at Old Maps & Prints

AUSTIN BUSH / LONELY PLANET IMAGES ©

NEIGHBOURHOODS

RIVERSIDE & SILOM

🖼 LIN SILVERCRAFT *Jewellery*
☎ 0 2235 2108; 14 Soi 40/Oriental, Th Charoen Krung; 🕙 9am-6pm Mon-Sat; 🚇 Saphan Taksin, 🚌 75, 504, ⛴ Tha Oriental; ♿
Lin might be a bit pricier than your average Bangkok silver shop but you know you're getting the genuine article. You can pick up classic pieces such as silver chokers, thick bangles and custom-engraved cuff links.

🖼 MAISON DES ARTS *Handicrafts*
☎ 0 2234 7547; 1334 Th Charoen Krung; 🕙 10am-6pm Mon-Sat; 🚇 Saphan Taksin, 🚌 75, 504, ⛴ Tha Oriental
Hand-hammered stainless-steel tableware haphazardly occupies this warehouse retail shop. The bold style of the flatware dates back centuries and the staff applies no pressure to indecisive shoppers.

🖼 OLD MAPS & PRINTS *Antiques*
☎ 0 2237 0077/8; www.classicmaps. com; 4th fl, River City, Th Yotha;

LOVE HURTS
Be careful before you start falling in love with images or statues of Buddha and other deities. For any image that isn't an amulet (intended for religious purposes), you'll need an export licence to take the object out of the country. Contact the Fine Arts Department at ☎ 0 2628 5032 for more information.

🕙 11am-7pm Mon-Sat, to 6pm Sun; 🚌 75, 504, ⛴ free shuttle boat from Tha Sathon; ♿
You could poke around in this shop for hours, flipping through the maps of Siam and Indochina, looking at early explorers' quaint drawings of 'the natives' and sighing with delight at the exquisite framed prints.

🖼 PATPONG NIGHT MARKET *Market*
Th Patpong; 🕙 6pm-2am; 🚇 Sala Daeng, Ⓜ Si Lom
The Patpong area is the ultimate Bangkok cliché, where everything

TAXING STUFF INDEED
You can claim back some of the VAT (value-added tax) you've paid but the requirements are a little tricky. To qualify, you must have spent at least 5000B on the goods, which must be bought at participating stores, where you have to show your passport and complete the appropriate forms. You also must have been in Thailand for fewer than 180 days in a calendar year, be leaving the country by plane and apply for a refund with goods in hand at the airport departure hall. See the VAT Refund for Tourists website (www.rd.go.th/vrt/howwill.html) to make sense of it all.

FAKING IT

Knocking off name-brand goods is a Bangkok speciality. Many say that these fakes are after-hours creations: once the factory officially closes, the machines keep going to feed the underground market. These name brands without quality control are the cream of the knock-off crop, while others are just copycats. It's all highly illegal, of course, and many Western manufacturers have long been pressuring the Thai government to get these goods off the street. But the grey market is tenacious at circumventing spotty enforcement. Now vendors only show off pictures of fake Rolexes to customers and once a deal has been sealed a runner delivers the goods in discreet packaging. The obvious similarities between buying drugs and fake goods is often lost on the upright citizens admiring their new wristwatches.

can be had for a price. In one corner are the famous circuslike sex shows and in the other is a crowded market selling all manner of name-brand knock-offs. (Make sure you bargain hard as prices here are grossly inflated.) And lying in ambush are the 'DVD, CVD, Sex' video sellers who pop up just as your wife has stepped past.

🏠 RIVER CITY *Shopping Centre*
☎ 0 2237 0077; off Th Yotha; 🕐 10am-10pm; 🚌 75, 504, 🚢 free shuttle boat from Tha Sathon; ♿
Only got time for one antique shop? This four-floor complex of art, antiques and auctioneers is a one-stop shop for a Burmese Buddha image, black silk or a *benjarong* (traditional royal Thai ceramics) tea set, and you pay for the quality. The stores can arrange to ship your buys back home.

🏠 SILOM VILLAGE TRADE CENTRE *Handicrafts*
286 Th Silom; 🕐 10am-9pm; 🚌 Surasak; 🚌 15, 504; ♿
It's blissfully easy to wander around this cluster of shops. While some vendors sell the ubiquitous touristy fare, the antique shops have carved teak wall decorations to turn your house into a traditional Thai home.

🏠 SOI LALAI SAP MARKET *Market*
Soi 5, Th Silom; 🕐 10am-3pm Mon-Fri; 🚌 Chong Nonsi; ♿
Literally 'the *soi* [lane] that melts your money away', at lunchtime this street is packed with Thai secretaries bargaining for fake handbags, homewares and polyester clothing. Rejects from brand-name factories in Cambodia sometimes make an appearance here.

🏠 S.V. JEWELERY *Jewellery*

☎ 0 2233 7347; 1254-6 Th Charoen Krung; ⏱ 10.30am-7pm Mon-Sat; 🚇 Saphan Taksin, 🚌 75, 504, ⚓ Tha Oriental; ♿

With a big showroom on bustling Th Charoen Krung, S.V. Jewelery isn't just a shop for girly baubles and body decorations. You'll find cuff links in all sizes, shapes and attitudes, silver elephants, enormous gleaming photo frames and key rings.

🏠 THAI HOME INDUSTRIES
Handicrafts

☎ 0 2234 1736; 35 Soi 40/Oriental, Th Charoen Krung; ⏱ 9am-6.30pm Mon-Sat; 🚇 Saphan Taksin, 🚌 75, 504, ⚓ Tha Oriental; ♿

You can wander at will around this enormous traditional Thai building overflowing with boxes. The staff leave you to your own devices to poke around the bronzeware, silverware (especially cutlery) and basketry.

🏠 THAVIBU GALLERY *Art*

☎ 0 2266 5454; www.thavibu.com; 3rd fl, Silom Galleria, 919/1 Th Silom; ⏱ 11am-7pm Mon-Sat, noon-6pm Sun; 🚇 Surasak, 🚌 15, 504; ♿

Young artists from Southeast Asia (namely Myanmar, Thailand and Vietnam) are showcased in this virtual and brick-and-mortar gallery. With a huge internet presence,

ART CONQUISTADORS

Folks crow about Thailand's great gem buys, but all the deals have been cornered by scammers. For savvy shoppers with a stash of cash, check out the great Thai contemporary-art buys. Asian art, especially from China and Vietnam, is all the rage with international buyers, and speculators have long had their eyes on the Southeast Asian art scene. The city's galleries specialise in all manner of wall hangings, from paint to prints, and open new exhibits with social parties where Bangkok's cliques trade name cards and musings on Thailand.

Check the English-language press for exhibition openings or visit the following galleries at quieter times: **Thavibu Gallery** (left), **H Gallery** (p97) and **Kathmandu Photo Gallery** (p94).

Thavibu cultivates a wide international audience and is a major resource of art and art information for the region.

🍴 EAT

Bangkok's financial district does a lot of wining and dining, especially geared towards tourists and businesspeople.

🍴 FOODIE *Thai* $$

☎ 0 2231 5278; 150 Soi Phiphat 2; ⏱ 11am-11pm Mon-Sat; 🚇 Chong Nonsi

This airy, cafeteria-like restaurant boasts a menu of hard-to-find

STRICTLY VEGETARIAN

It's tough to be truly vegetarian at Thai restaurants. You can ask for 'no meat or seafood' but then your dish arrives with fish sauce. But you won't need to worry at strictly vegetarian places such as **Arawy** (p58) and the vegetarian stall at the **MBK Food Court** (p88) or Indian restaurants such as **Dosa King** (p126) and **Indian Hut** (below). Don't miss Chinatown during its annual Vegetarian Festival.

central- and southern-style Thai dishes. Highlights here include Yam som o (which is a spicy/ sour/sweet pomelo salad) and the spicy Prik khing pla dook foo (catfish fried in a curry paste until crispy).

🍴 INDIAN HUT *North Indian* $$$

☎ 0 2635 7876; 311/2-5 Th Surawong; 🕙 11am-11pm; 🚌 75, 504, 🚢 Tha Oriental; 👶 Ⓥ

We can't stress it enough: don't walk out the door of Indian Hut without first tasting its delectable homemade cottage cheese, preferably sampled as part of the deceptively simple tomato-and-onion curry. Despite the fast-food overtones in the name of the restaurant, this place is very classy and is popular with businesspeople.

🍴 KALPAPRUEK RESTAURANT *Thai* $$

☎ 0 2236 4335; 27 Th Pramuan, Th Silom; 🕙 8am-6pm Mon-Sat, to 3pm Sun; 🚇 Surasak

This venerable Thai eatery has numerous branches and mall spin-offs around town, but we still fancy the quasi-concealed original branch. The diverse menu spans specialities from just about every region of Thailand, and has daily specials and, occasionally, seasonal treats.

🍴 KRUA 'AROY-AROY' *Thai* $

☎ 0 2635 2365; Th Pan; 🕙 8am-8.30pm, closed 2nd & 4th Sun of each month; 🚌 15, 504, 🚇 Surasak

Family-run 'Delicious Kitchen' rarely fails to live up to its moniker. Stop by for some of Bangkok's richest curries, as well as daily specials such as *kôw klúk gà·bì* (rice cooked with shrimp paste and served with a variety of toppings).

🍴 LE NORMANDIE *French* $$$

☎ 0 2659 9000; Oriental Hotel, 48 Soi 40/Oriental, Th Charoen Krung; 🕙 noon-3pm & 7-11pm Mon-Sat, 7-11pm Sun; 🚇 Saphan Taksin, 🚌 75, 504, 🚢 free shuttle boat from Tha Sathon; 👶

Give yourself time to prepare for Le Normandie, one of Bangkok's finest. Make sure the jacket and tie are dry-cleaned and the booking is confirmed. Discipline your stomach and get your mind ready for some big decisions: the dégustation or roast lobster with handmade egg noodles and bisque sauce? Leave room for the scrumptious raspberry gratin crowned with an ice cream of raspberry liqueur.

🍴 MIZU'S KITCHEN *Japanese* $$
☎ 0 2233 6447; 32 Soi Patpong 1, Th Silom; ⌚ noon-midnight; 🚉 Sala Daeng, Ⓜ Si Lom; ♿ ♨

Warm and salty, Mizu's fusion of Japanese and American dishes is the perfect nightcap after a schedule of heavy drinking. Although your reflexes might be dulled, use the red-and-white chequered tablecloth to screen yourself from the soy sauce–hissing hotplates.

🍴 NAAZ *Thai-Muslim* $
☎ 0 2234 4537; 24/9 Soi 45, Th Charoen Krung; ⌚ 8.30am-10pm Mon-Sat; 🚌 75, 504; ⚓ Tha Oriental

Hidden in a nondescript alleyway is Naaz (pronounced *nát*), a tiny

living-room kitche of the city's riches (chicken biriani). Various daily specials include chicken masala and mutton korma, but we're most curious to visit on Thursdays when the restaurant serves something called Karai Ghost.

🍴 NADIMOS *Lebanese* $$
☎ 0 2266 9081; www.nadimos.com; Baan Silom, cnr Th Silom & Soi 19; ⌚ 11am-11.30pm; 🚉 Surasak, 🚌 15, 504; ♿ Ⓥ

This semiformal dining room does tasty versions of all the Lebanese standards, plus quite a few dishes you'd never expect to see this far from Beirut. Lots of vegetarian options as well.

🍴 SCOOZI *Italian* $$
☎ 0 2234 6999; www.scoozipizza.com; 174 Th Surawong; ⌚ 10.30am-10.30pm; 🚉 Sala Daeng, Ⓜ Si Lom; ♿ ♨ Ⓥ

There are several Scoozis across Bangkok, but we think the wood-fired pizzas taste best at the original branch. Go minimalist and try the *napoletana*, rendered

IN THE KNOW
Need to know the hottest new restaurant or the latest chic bar? Bangkok morphs more quickly than the print before you, so to keep up seek out listing mags *Bangkok 101* (www.bangkok101.com), a stylish monthly magazine following new openings and happenings, and *BK* (www.bkmagazine.com), available free at bars and restaurants. Online, CNNGo's Bangkok pages (www.cnngo.com/bangkok) are a good source of all-round info, while Bangkok Recorder (www.bangkokrecorder.com) watches the DJ scene.

satisfyingly briny by the addition of black olives and anchovies. Pasta, salads, gelati and other desserts are also available.

🍴 SOI 10 FOOD CENTRES
Thai $

Soi 10, Th Silom; ⏱ **9am-2pm Mon-Fri;** 🚇 **Chong Nonsi;** ♿ **Ⓥ**

These two adjacent hangarlike buildings tucked behind Soi 10 are the main lunchtime fuelling stations for Bangkok's unofficial financial district. Choices range from authentic southern-style *kôw gaang* (point-and-choose curries ladled over rice) to virtually every kind of Thai noodle, and even a few vegie options.

🍴 SOMBOON SEAFOOD
Chinese Seafood $$$

☎ **0 2234 3104; 169/7-11 Th Surawong;** ⏱ **4-11.30pm;** 🚇 **Chong Nonsi;** ♿ ♿ **Ⓥ**

Holy seafood factory: ascending the many staircases to a free table might make you nervous about the quality of so much quantity. But Somboon Seafood's famous crab curry is bound to make you messy and full. Dainty eaters can opt for the slightly more surgical pursuit of devouring a whole fried fish.

🍴 SOMTAM CONVENT
Northeastern Thai $

☎ **0 2634 2839; 2/4-5 Th Convent;** ⏱ **10.30am-9pm;** 🚇 **Sala Daeng,** Ⓜ **Si Lom**

CRUISING FOR DINNER

Dinner cruises sail along the Mae Nam Chao Phraya at night, far away from the heat and noise of the city but basking in the twinkling lights. These floating buffets range from sophisticated to home style and several cruise underneath Saphan Phra Ram IX, the longest single-span cable-suspension bridge in the world. The food of course runs a distant second to the ambience.

Yok Yor Marina & Restaurant (☎ 0 2863 0565; www.yokyor.co.th; 885 Soi Somdet Chao Phraya 17, Thonburi; dinner à la carte plus surcharge 140/70B; ⏱ 8-10pm; 🚤 river-crossing ferry from Tha Si Phraya) is a favourite among Thais celebrating birthdays.

Wan Fah Cruises (☎ 0 2222 8679; www.wanfah.in.th; River City shopping complex; dinner cruises 1200B; ⏱ 7-9pm; 🚤 river taxi to Tha Si Phraya) is a buxom wooden boat with Thai music and traditional dance.

Manohra Cruises (off Map p134; ☎ 0 2476 0022; www.manohracruises.com; Bangkok Marriott Resort & Spa, Thonburi; dinner cruises 1400-1990B; ⏱ 7.30-10pm; free hotel shuttle from Tha Sathon) commands a fleet of converted teak barges that part the waters with regal flair.

HIGH TEA

High tea is such an institution in Bangkok, you'd have thought Thailand was colonised. Tea in the **Oriental Hotel's Author's Lounge** (☎ 0 2659 9000; 48 Soi 40/Oriental, Th Charoen Krung; high tea 1236B; ☼ noon-6pm; ⛴ Saphan Taksin, 🚌 75, 504, ⛴ free shuttle boat from Tha Sathon) is right out of a Victorian story book, with potted plants, cane furniture and tiered silver servers.

If you think brewed leaves are best left to Miss Marple, break the mid-day with the chocolate buffet at the **Sukhothai Hotel** (Map p109, B4; ☎ 0 2344 8888; 13 Th Sathon Tai; high tea 800B; ☼ 2-5.30pm Fri-Sun; Ⓜ Lumphini).

Tea time is usually between 2pm and 6pm.

Northeastern-style Thai food is usually relegated to less-than-hygienic stalls that are perched by the side of the road and have no menu or English-speaking staff in sight. A less-intimidating intro to the wonders of *lâhp* (a 'salad' of minced meat), *sôm·dam* (papaya salad) and other Isan delights can be had at this popular restaurant.

🍴 TALING PLING *Thai* $$
☎ 0 2230 4830; 60 Th Pan; ☼ 11am-11pm; Ⓜ Surasak
You know you've picked well when Thai families outnumber expats. And you get a stylish setting. A few menu standouts include *yam ɓlah sà·lìt đà·ling ɓling* (a fried-fish salad with the namesake sour vegetable), chicken wrapped in pandanus leaves and *pàt pàk đam·leung* (stir-fried gourd leaves). Located off Th Silom.

 DRINK
Lower Silom is Bangkok's gaybourhood. The *soi* around Patpong undergo various surges in popularity as a drinking-and-clubbing scene. Even if things are in a slump, you'll still need to wet your whistle after bargaining at the Patpong Night Market.

🍸 BALCONY BAR *Gay & Lesbian*
☎ 0 2235 5891; www.balconypub.com; 86-88 Soi 4, Th Silom; ☼ 5.30pm-2am; Ⓜ Sala Daeng, Ⓜ Si Lom; ♿
Balcony is a classic good-time bar, where hot pants and string vests check out the talent and tables of straight couples order countless rounds. An outside table under the lanterns is the prime position for watching the passing parade.

STRAIGHT TO THE MOON

You have to be high to think that Bangkok is beautiful. High in altitude, that is. Locals love to show off their overgrown town from the rooftop bars that pair tummy butterflies with cocktails. Toast the town from these rooftop bars, which both have a smart casual dress code: **Sirocco & Sky Bar** (below) and **Moon Bar at Vertigo** (p112).

▼ BAMBOO BAR *Live Music*
☎ 0 2659 9000; Oriental Hotel, 48 Soi 40/Oriental, Th Charoen Krung; ◷ 11am-1am; ⊞ Saphan Taksin, ⊟ 75, 504, ⛴ free shuttle boat from Tha Sathon; ♿
You could be forgiven for thinking that Thailand was a British colony when you visit the Bamboo Bar, the city's top jazz spot. Patrons sip G&Ts while lounging in rattan chairs, feeling a million miles away from the heat and dust, while jazz bands or singers soothe any remaining tensions.

▼ SIROCCO & SKY BAR *Bar*
☎ 0 2624 9555; The Dome, 1055 Th Silom; ◷ 6pm-1am; ⊞ Saphan Taksin
Descend the sweeping stairs like a Hollywood diva to the precipice bar of this rooftop restaurant. A dress code is enforced and drink prices are impressive, but so is the view.

▼ TELEPHONE *Gay & Lesbian*
☎ 0 2234 3279; www.telephonepub.com; 114/11 Soi 4, Th Silom; ◷ 5pm-1am; ⊞ Sala Daeng, ◉ Si Lom
Muscle boys and queens parade past the outdoor tables at Telephone, one of Bangkok's oldest, most popular gay bars.

★ PLAY

☆ DJ STATION *Gay & Lesbian*
☎ 0 2266 4029; 8/6-8 Soi 2, Th Silom; ◷ 10pm-late; ⊞ Sala Daeng, ◉ Si Lom
Neoindustrial DJ Station is a longstanding dance club in a town that loves change. The music varies wildly from handbag to hard house but the dance floor remains packed with shirtless sweaty boys. If you don't like the scene here, this tiny *soi* has an avenue's worth of options so move along and take your pick.

☆ G.O.D. *Gay & Lesbian*
☎ 0 2632 8032; Soi 2/1, Th Silom; ◷ 10pm-late; ⊞ Sala Daeng, ◉ Si Lom
As the name suggests, Guys On Display has nothing against a bit of shirtless dancing. It's open late, too.

☆ SALA RIM NAAM *Theatre*
☎ 0 2659 9000; Oriental Hotel, 48 Soi 40/Oriental, Th Charoen Krung; tickets 2649B; ◷ shows 8.20-9.20pm; ⊞ Saphan Taksin, ⊟ 75, 504, ⛴ free shuttle boat from Tha Sathon; ♿ ⛐

Meeker now, but the red lights still flicker in infamous Patpong

RICHARD I'ANSON / LONELY PLANET IMAGES ©

Riverside Sala Rim Naam, a stunning Thai pavilion made of teak, marble and bronze, holds nightly classical-dance performances preceded by a set Thai meal. Part of the Oriental Hotel cultural program.

TAPAS ROOM *Dance Club*
☎ 0 2234 4737; www.tapasroom.net; 114/17-18 Soi 4, Th Silom; admission

200B; ☽ 10pm-3am; ⓧ Sala Daeng, ⊖ Si Lom

When patrons first arrive, this Moorish-style bar is mellow, with wavering candlelight. Everyone lies back against big cushions, nodding to the chilled-out house beats. Later the disco ball starts swirling and the dance floor gets sweaty.

>LUMPHINI

Just when Bangkok seemed hopelessly congested, foresighted city officials preserved Lumphini Park as the city's central green space in the 1920s. The tropical heat shoos away visitors during the day but the cooler temperatures of the morning and evening bring out Bangkokians' sporty side.

The area surrounding the park is prime real estate for foreign embassies on the divided roadway of Th Sathon. Closer to the park is a resuscitated nightspot of itsy-bitsy clubs on Th Sarasin. Th Phra Ram IV is one of Bangkok's bulkiest thoroughfares, with a traffic flyover that provides one of the best views of the city from a car window. Branching off Th Phra Ram IV is the ageing backpacker scene around Soi Ngam Duphli. The Lumphini MRT station has made it easier to get in and out of the area, which is otherwise strangled by uncrossable intersections and relentless traffic.

LUMPHINI

◎ SEE
Lumphini Park 1 B2

🏃 DO
Banyan Tree Spa 2 B4

🍴 EAT
Café 1912 .... 3 B4
D'Sens 4 A3
nahm 5 B4
Ngwanlee Lang Suan 6 C1
Soi Polo Fried Chicken ... 7 D2
Sukhothai Hotel ....(see 8)

🍸 DRINK
Moon Bar at Vertigo ... (see 2)
Sukhothai Hotel 8 B4
Wong's Place 9 D5

★ PLAY
70s Bar 10 B1
Brown Sugar 11 B1
Lumphini Boxing
  Stadium 12 D4

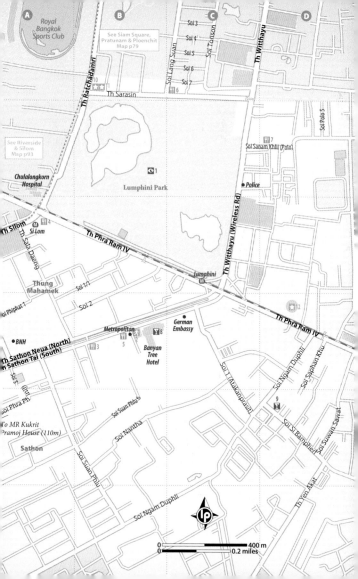

SEE

LUMPHINI PARK

Th Phra Ram IV; admission free;
4.30am-9pm; Sala Daeng,
Lumphini or Si Lom;
Bangkok's biggest central park,
located between Th Witthayu and
Th Ratchadamri, has nurtured
many a bike rider, jogger, *đà·gròr*
(a Thai football game) player and
t'ai chi practitioner. After developing the Bangkok cough, try a few
gulps of fresh air at Lumphini.

AUSTIN BUSH / LONELY PLANET IMAGES ©

Wok magic: savour the city's best street food

MR KUKRIT PRAMOJ HOUSE

0 2287 2937; Soi 7, Th Narathiwat
Ratchanakharin; admission 50/20B;
10am-4pm; Chong Nonsi
Mom Ratchawong Kukrit Pramoj
once resided in this complex.
European-educated but devoutly
Thai, MR Kukrit surrounded himself
with the best of both worlds: five
traditional teak buildings, Thai art,
Western books and lots of heady
conversations. A guided tour offers
a more intimate introduction to
the former resident, who authored
more than 150 books and served
as prime minister of Thailand.

DO

BANYAN TREE SPA *Spa*

0 2679 1052; www.banyantree.com;
Banyan Tree Hotel, 21/100 Th Sathon Tai;
day packages from 5000B; 9am-
10pm; Lumphini;
This 21st-floor spa is one of the
most luxurious in the city. Decked
out in new-millennium tranquillity,
the spa uses deep-tissue massages,
body wraps in warming spices
and a flower-bath to transport you
further into the beyond.

EAT

CAFÉ 1912 *French* $$

0 2679 2056; Alliance Française, 29
Th Sathon Tai; 7am-7pm Mon-Sat, to
2pm Sun; Lumphini; V

This congenial cafeteria, part of the French cultural centre, is a great place for *cuisine Française* without straining the budget. A few Thai dishes, good coffee, and delicious cakes and sweets, provided by a local bakery, are also available.

D'SENS *French* $$$
☎ 0 2200 9000; 22nd fl, Dusit Thani, 946 Th Phra Ram IV; noon-3pm & 6-11pm; Sala Daeng, Si Lom; V

Atop the Dusit Thani, overlooking Lumphini Park, this is a venture of French wonder-twins Laurent and Jacques Pourcel, creators of the Michelin-starred Le Jardin des Sens in Montpellier, France. The restaurant is handsome yet modern and the menu draws from the traditions of the south of France, relying mainly

---

FEEDING THE SPIRITS

The small houses that sit in front of homes and businesses aren't for child's play but for paranormal comfort. Known as spirit houses, these structures are intended for a site's guardian spirit. Daily offerings of joss sticks, flower garlands, fruit or a set of three small bowls (containing rice, sweetmeats and water) are set out to keep the spirit sated and to ensure the flow of good fortune.

---

on high-quality French imports for its ingredients.

NAHM *Thai* $$$
☎ 0 2625 3333; Metropolitan Hotel, 27 Th Sathon Tai; 7pm-midnight; Lumphini; V

This, the recently opened Bangkok branch of Australian chef David

---

STREET FOOD

Eating like a Thai means grabbing a plastic chair beside a little vendor cart or an outdoor market. Below are a few street-food recommendations and tips on spotting their purveyors. The books *Thai Hawker Food* and *Bangkok's Top 50 Street Food Stalls* (both available at most Bangkok bookstores) are also good starting points for getting your bearings for street food.

> *sôm-đam* (green papaya salad) – look for a large wooden mortar and order it with *khâo nĭaw* (sticky rice)
> *pàt tai* (thin rice noodles with tofu, vegetables, egg and peanuts) – any vendor with a wok can make this, but quality varies
> *kŭaytĭaw phàt khĭi mao* (literally 'drunkard's noodles'; wide rice noodles combined with meat, vegetables, chilli and Thai basil) – another wok wonder
> *khâo phàt* (stir-fried rice) – also available from wok vendors
> *khâo man kài* (chicken and rice) – look for carcasses of boiled chicken in the display case

Thompson's famed London restaurant, is hands-down the best upscale Thai in town. The expansive set menu spans both Thailand's regions and history, and will most likely cause you to look at all subsequent Thai meals with a critical eye.

🍴 NGWANLEE LANG SUAN
Thai $$

☎ 0 2250 0936; cnr Soi Lang Suan & Th Sarasin; 🕑 7am-3am; 🚇 Ratchadamri; **V**
This old-school food hall is a great place to try Thai-Chinese staples such as *jàp chǎi* (stewed vegies) or *bèt đun* (duck in Chinese spices). There's no air-con, but it's open late – perfect after a night on the town.

🍴 SOI POLO FRIED CHICKEN
Thai $$

☎ 0 2655 8489; 137/1-2 Soi Sanam Khlii (Polo), Th Witthayu; 🕑 10am-10pm; 🚇 Phloen Chit, 🚇 Lumphini; ♿ 👶

Your nose will lead you to what many claim is the best *gài tôrt* (fried chicken) in town; it certainly slaps down KFC. It's golden and crispy on the outside with lots of fried garlic bits. One half-order will generously feed two. Eat like a local: order sticky rice and employ the spicy dipping sauces.

🍸 DRINK

🍸 MOON BAR AT VERTIGO *Bar*

☎ 0 2679 1200; Banyan Tree Hotel, 21/100 Th Sathon Tai; 🕑 5.30pm-1am; 🚇 Lumphini
This sky-high, open-air bar will literally take your breath away. The elevator delivers you to the 59th floor of the Banyan Tree Hotel, where you weave your way through dimly lit hallways to the roar of Bangkok traffic far below. Come at sunset and gravitate to the right of the bar for more impressive views.

EAT YOUR HEART OUT
An eating contest with class? Indeed, the decadent hotel buffets push moderate eaters into overdrive as they make several laps through the stations loaded with seafood, braised meats, sashimi, raw oysters and a chocolate fountain. Most brunches are on Sunday from 11.30am to 3pm; call for details and advance reservations.

Royal Orchid Sheraton (Map p93, B2; ☎ 0 2266 0123; Soi 30/Captain Bush, Th Charoen Krung; buffets 1520-1990B) has a scenic riverside setting and enough kid's activities to feed families with food and fun. **Four Seasons Hotel** (Map p79, C3; ☎ 0 2250 1000; Th Ratchadamri; buffets 2120-2770B) generously fills a foie gras counter, free-flowing champagne and a decadent price tag. **Sukhothai Hotel** (☎ 0 2344 8888; 13 Th Sathon Tai; buffets 2590B) hosts a weekend brunch with free-flowing wines and all the fixings.

HIGH KICKS

The most dynamic and exciting Thai sport is *muay thai*, or Thai boxing, considered by many to be the ultimate in hand-to-hand fighting. Matches can be violent, but the surrounding spectacle of crazy music, prematch rituals and manic betting is half the draw. When a Thai boxer is ready for the ring, he is given a fighting name – usually a none-too-subtle reminder of how much pain these guys aim to inflict. Just so you know what you might be in for, recent clashes pitted such fighters as Dangerous Uneven-Legged Man vs the Bloody Elbow; the Human Stone vs the King of the Knee; and No Mercy Killer vs the Golden Left Leg. Fights are held at **Ratchadamnoen Boxing Stadium** (p63) and at **Lumphini Boxing Stadium** (below).

WONG'S PLACE *Bar*

27/3 Soi Si Bamphen; ⏰ 8pm-late;
🚇 Lumphini

A relic from the backpacker world of the early 1980s, Wong's Place (off Soi Ngam Duphli) is a homey after-hours drinking spot with an old-school soundtrack.

⭐ PLAY

⭐ 70S BAR *Gay & Lesbian*

☎ 0 2253 4433; Th Sarasin; ⏰ 6pm-1am; 🚇 Ratchadamri

This funky little closet is the remaining holdout of what was formerly one of Bangkok's pinkest strips. The '70s theme is in name only, but this doesn't seem to deter the disco-minded crowds who fill it up every weekend.

⭐ BROWN SUGAR *Live Music*

☎ 0 2250 1825; 231/20 Th Sarasin; ⏰ 5pm-1am; 🚇 Ratchadamri

Evoking the intimacy of New Orleans jazz clubs, this compact bar lends an ear to bebop and ragtime, leaving the smooth sounds to the hotel lobbies. On Sunday nights, the high-powered musicians who are touring the luxury hotels assemble here for impromptu jam sessions.

⭐ LUMPHINI BOXING STADIUM *Muay Thai*

☎ 0 2251 4303; Th Phra Ram IV; 🚇 Lumphini

Big-time *muay thai* fighters spar at Lumphini's coveted ring. Matches are on Tuesday and Friday at 6.30pm and Saturday at 5pm and 8.30pm. Tickets are 1000/1500/2000B (3rd class/2nd class/ringside). The stadium doesn't usually fill up until the main event around 8pm. For a few years there's been talk of the stadium moving to Th Nang Linji but, at research time, a decision had not been made.

>SUKHUMVIT

The most urban and cosmopolitan part of Bangkok, Th Sukhumvit arches from the alleged centre of the city all the way to the Gulf of Thailand. Along the lower-numbered *soi* (lanes), the street is home to a thriving sex- tourism scene (namely Nana Entertainment Plaza and Soi Cowboy), while the city's elite live and play at the more respectable upper end. Every version of accomplished expat – from formerly exiled aristocratic Thais to Japanese executives – claims a Sukhumvit address, and the commercial corridor caters to these big-budget tastes.

The money-hungry pursuits of shopping, bar-hopping and fashionable dining will occupy a Sukhumvit outing. A more down-home activity is a visit to Bangkok's Little Arabia, crammed into Soi 3/1. Hummus not curry

SUKHUMVIT

◉ SEE
Ban Kamthieng 1 C3
Benjasiri Park 2 D4
Chuvit Garden 3 B2
Khlong Toey Market 4 B6
Thailand Creative &
    Design Center ....(see 12)

🏃 DO
Asia Herb
    Association ....(see 38)
Coran Boutique Spa 5 B1
Divana Massage & Spa ..6 C3
Rasayana Retreat 7 E3
Salon de Bkk ....(see 12)
Take Care 8 C2
World Fellowship of
    Buddhists ....(see 2)

🏠 SHOP
Almeta 9 C2
Asia Books 10 B2
Dasa Book Café 11 E4
Emporium 12 D4

Greyhound ....(see 12)
Jaspal ....(see 12)
Jim Thompson ....(see 12)
Kinokuniya Books ......(see 12)
Nandakwang 13 D2
Nickermann's Tailors ..14 A2
Phu Fa 15 B2
Propaganda ....(see 12)
Raja's Fashions 16 A2
Villa Market 17 D4

🍴 EAT
Bed Supperclub 18 B1
Bei Otto 19 D3
Bharani 20 C2
Bo.lan 21 E5
Boon Tong Kiat
    Singapore Hainanese
    Chicken Rice 22 G3
Cabbages & Condoms ..23 B3
Crêpes & Co 24 B3
Dosa King 25 B2
Face 26 G6
Federal Hotel Coffee
    Shop 27 B1

Kuppa 28 C4
Le Beaulieu 29 C2
Myeong Ga 30 B2
Nasir Al-Masri
    Restaurant 31 A1
Rosabieng 32 B2
Soi 38 Night Market ..33 G6

🍸 DRINK
Bangkok Bar 34 H6
Bull's Head 35 D4
Cheap Charlie's 36 B2
Iron Fairies 37 G3
Soul Food Mahanakorn 38 G5
Titanium 39 D4
WTF 40 F5

⭐ PLAY
Bed Supperclub ......(see 18)
Ekamai Soi 5 ....41 H4
Living Room 42 C3
Nung-Len 43 H4
Q Bar 44 B1
SFX Cinema ....(see 12)

Please see over for map

114

dominates the restaurant menus and most customers stop in to bubble the water pipes and catch up on Al Jazeera.

Although Sukhumvit is an endless traffic jam, the BTS train system makes plenty of far-flung spots more accessible.

◉ SEE
◉ BAN KAMTHIENG

☎ 0 2661 6470; Siam Society, 131 Soi 21 (Asoke), Th Sukhumvit; admission 100/50B; ⏲ 9am-5pm Tue-Sat; ⛟ Asok, ◉ Sukhumvit

Ban Kamthieng is an excellent merging of pretty architecture with museum learning. Built in the Lanna style, this 1844 house shows how a northern Thai family lived, complete with thorough explanations of Lanna beliefs, rituals and ceremonies. This is one of Bangkok's best house museums and has well-signed displays, video installations and clear descriptions of rituals. Plus you never have to share space with others.

◉ BENJASIRI PARK

Th Sukhumvit; admission free; ⏲ 5am-8pm; ⛟ Phrom Phong; ♿
In summer this park, built to honour Queen Sirikit's 60th birthday, hosts many open-air events. Set around an ornamental lake, most of the surrounding lawn space is taken by canoodling couples and teenage mating rituals-in-progress. If you're lucky you might spy a game of đà·grôr (a Thai football game played with a rattan ball).

◉ CHUVIT GARDEN

Th Sukhumvit; admission free; ⏲ 6-10am & 4-8pm; ⛟ Nana; ♿
The story behind this park is shadier than the plantings. Khun Chuvit, the benefactor of the park, was Bangkok's biggest massage-parlour owner. He was arrested in 2003 for

---

SHORT-TERM CHAUFFEURS

Strolling Sukhumvit's *soi* (lanes) that branch off the main avenue can be a real drag. There's no clear footpath, shade or safety from speeding cars. And if you look around, only foreigners and pushcart vendors even try walking these obstacle courses. Thais hop aboard the motorcycle taxis that sit at the mouth of the *soi* just for this purpose. You too can be spared from heat exhaustion by naming your destination or the point within the *soi* – *sòot soi* (end of the *soi*), *glahng soi* (middle of the soi) or *bàhk soi* (mouth of the *soi*) – and climbing aboard the back of the bike. These little hops cost 10B; don't bother to ask the price as some drivers will be creative with their answers.

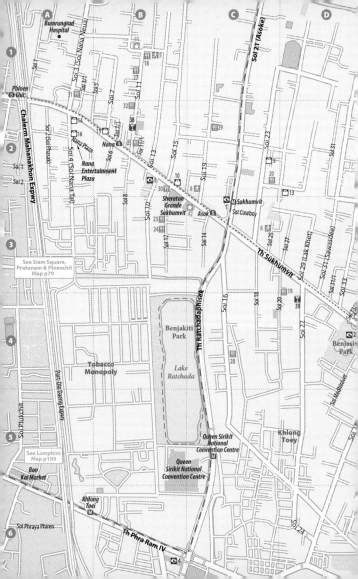

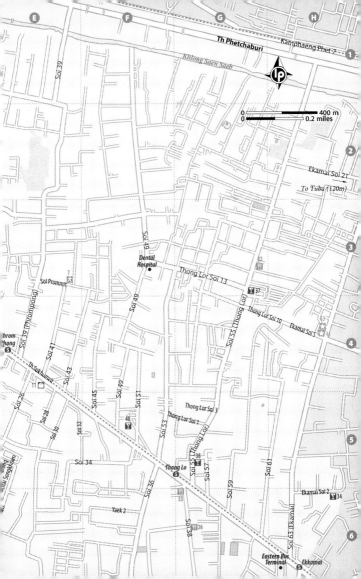

illegally bulldozing, rather than legally evicting, tenants off the land where the park now stands (between Soi 8 and 10). With all the media attention, he sang like a bird about the police bribes he handed out during his career and became an unlikely activist against police corruption. Chuvit later ran unsuccessfully for Bangkok governor in 2004 and successfully for the Thai parliament in 2005. This park was one of his campaign promises. It's a pretty, green patch in a neighbourhood lean on trees.

 KHLONG TOEY MARKET
cnr Th Ratchadaphisek & Th Phra Ram IV; 5-10am; Khlong Toei

This wholesale market – one of the city's largest – is the likely origin of

many of the meals you'll eat while in Bangkok.

THAILAND CREATIVE & DESIGN CENTER
☎ 0 2664 8448; www.tcdc.or.th; 6th fl, Emporium, Th Sukhumvit; admission free; 10.30am-9pm Tue-Sun; Phrom Phong;

An edu-tainment museum and resource centre, the TCDC spotlights modern design from famous fashion houses to image-branding products. Past exhibits have included a history of the Finnish company Marimekko as well as a retrospective of cool gadgets. The intention of the centre is to foster and inspire Thailand's fledgling industry of industrial design.

Retro meets modern at the Thailand Creative & Design Center

A DATE WITH A DOCTOR

Most holidaymakers hope not to end up in hospital, but these days Thailand has become a destination for medical treatments, from hip replacements to nips and tucks. It's cheaper, and offers better service and often more sophisticated technology. Here are a few of the hospitals that cater to Westerners:

BNH (Map p109, A4; ☎ 0 2686 2700; www.bnhhospital.com; Th Convent; 🚇 Sala Daeng, 🔵 Si Lom) Well regarded for general medicine and dental procedures.

Bumrungrad Hospital (Map p116, A1; ☎ 0 2667 1000; www.bumrungrad.com; 33 Soi 3, Th Sukhumvit; 🚇 Nana) Blends five-star service and hotel-style accommodation with US-managed and -accredited medical facilities.

Dental Hospital (Map p116, F3; ☎ 0 2260 5000; www.dentalhospitalbangkok.com; 88/88 Soi 49, Th Sukhumvit; ⏱ 9am-8pm Mon-Sat, to 4pm Sun; 🚇 Phrom Phong) A private dental clinic that covers regular check-ups, fillings and root canals.

St Carlos Medical Spa (off Map p134; ☎ 0 2975 6700; www.stcarlos.com; Krung Siam St Carlos Medical Center, 5/84 Moo 2, Th Tiwanon, Banklang, Pathum Thani; 🚇 Mo Chit & access by taxi) For the noncelebrity hooked on celebrity treatments, such as detoxifying and fasting programs using traditional Thai medicines and massage.

Yanhee Hospital (Map p134, B2; ☎ 0 2879 0300; www.yanhee.net; 454 Th Charoen Sanit Wong; 🚇 Victory Monument & access by taxi) A blessing for every Tom, Dick and Harry who'd rather be Jane. The hospital specialises in sex reassignment and chondroplasty (shaving of the Adam's apple) without the long waiting lists that accompany such procedures overseas.

DO

🏃 ASIA HERB ASSOCIATION
Spa

☎ 0 2392 3631; www.asiaherbassocia tion.com; 58/19-25 Soi 55 (Thong Lor), Th Sukhumvit; Thai massage per hr 350B; ⏱ 9am-midnight; 🚇 Thong Lo

This Japanese-owned chain specialises in massage using *bràkòp* (traditional Thai herbal compresses filled with 18 different herbs).

🏃 CORAN BOUTIQUE SPA *Spa*

☎ 0 2651 1588; www.coranbangkok. com; 27/1-2 Soi 13, Th Sukhumvit; Thai massage per hr 400B; ⏱ 11am-10pm; 🚇 Nana; ♿

Located in an attractively refurbished home, this pint-sized spa offers traditional Thai massage and other spa treatments.

🏃 DIVANA MASSAGE & SPA *Spa*

☎ 0 2261 6784; www.divanaspa.com; 7 Soi 25, Th Sukhumvit; massages from 1500B; ⏱ 11am-11pm Mon-Fri, 10am-11pm Sat & Sun; 🚇 Asok, 🔵 Sukhumvit

Divana emphasises Thai massage and body scrubs as well as exotic beauty treatments. The menu might look familiar but the setting

119

NEIGHBOURHOODS

SUKHUMVIT

HAIRY SITUATION

Bangkok is all about hair. The socialites wear it long and straight without a hint of frizz. They worship at the various salons owned by Somsak Chulachol, stylists to the stars, including **Salon de Bkk** (☎ 0 2664 8880; 1st fl, Emporium, Th Sukhumvit; 🕑 10am-9pm; 🚇 Phrom Phong). The hip teens go for that special breed of Asian mullet at **Chic Club** (Map p79, B2; ☎ 0 2658 4147; Soi 5, Siam Square, Th Phra Ram I; 🕑 10am-8pm; 🚇 Siam). For no-nonsense gals, there's reliable **Take Care** (☎ 0 2254 4780; 19/31 Soi 19, Th Sukhumvit; 🕑 10am-8pm Mon-Sat; 🚇 Asok), where you get a sensible do and a nice chat.

is touchingly Thai: an atmospheric villa and lush garden so typical of Sukhumvit estates.

✈ RASAYANA RETREAT *Spa*
☎ 0 2662 4803; www.rasayanaretreat.com; 57 Soi Prommit off Soi 39, Th Sukhumvit; massages from 1600B; 🕑 10am-7pm; 🚇 Phrom Phong
The latest generation of spa facilities, Rasayana combines basic beauty and massage treatments with holistic healing techniques such as detoxification, colonic irrigation and hypnotherapy.

✈ WORLD FELLOWSHIP OF BUDDHISTS *Meditation*
☎ 0 2661 1284; www.wfb-hq.org; Benjasiri Park, Th Sukhumvit; admission free; 🕑 8.30am-4pm Sun-Fri; 🚇 Phrom Phong; ♿
On the first Sunday of the month, this centre of Theravada Buddhism hosts meditation classes in English from 2pm to 5pm. The fellowship also holds interesting forums on Buddhist issues.

🛍 SHOP

Looking for a reputable tailor or high-end fashion? Well, you've come to the right neighbourhood. If you need more pedestrian items you're also in the right place – Th Sukhumvit's souvenir market stretches from Soi 2 to Soi 12, and Soi 3 to Soi 15, every day except Monday.

🛍 ALMETA *Fashion*
☎ 0 2204 1413; www.almeta.com; 20/3 Soi 23, Th Sukhumvit; 🕑 9am-6pm; 🚇 Asok, Ⓜ Sukhumvit; ♿
If the colours of Thai silk evoke frumpy society matrons, then you're a candidate for Almeta's toned-down earth tones similar in hue to raw sugar or lotus blossoms.

🛍 ASIA BOOKS *Books*
☎ 0 2664 8545; Th Sukhumvit; 🕑 8am-9pm; 🚇 Asok, Ⓜ Sukhumvit
Bangkok's homegrown English-language bookstore has a stand-alone shop along busy Th Sukhumvit. It also has branches in Emporium (p121), Siam Paragon

(p86) and Siam Discovery Center (p86) shopping centres.

📷 DASA BOOK CAFÉ *Books*
☎ 0 2661 2993; Th Sukhumvit;
🕐 10am-8pm; 🚇 Phrom Phong; ♿

This humble shop is one of a handful of independent English-language bookstores to be found in town. Come in to peruse the used tomes, including many titles in languages other than English, or just stop by for coffee and cake.

🏛 EMPORIUM *Shopping Centre*
☎ 0 2664 7100; Th Sukhumvit;
🕐 10am-10pm; 🚇 Phrom Phong; ♿

This top-flight mall cleverly woos young urban princesses and matronly aristocrats by stocking the hippest of fashion designers

(Miu Miu, Prada), hardcore luxury brands (Chanel, Rolex) and classy eateries (Greyhound Café, Salon de l'Oriental). Despite the catwalk sauntering of these high-society bag girls, it all comes together without a stitch of intimidation.

🏛 GREYHOUND *Fashion*
☎ 0 2260 7121; www.greyhound. co.th; 2nd fl, Emporium, Th Sukhumvit;
🕐 10am-10pm; 🚇 Phrom Phong; ♿

Greyhound makes sleek streetwear – basics with an edge – for urbanites. Like many fashion houses, it has expanded to become a lifestyle brand that includes mini-malist cafes and spin-off brands (Playhound and Grey). Also in Siam Center (p86) and Siam Paragon (p86) shopping centres.

There's no end of beautiful bits in the Emporium's speciality shops

RICHARD I'ANSON / LONELY PLANET IMAGES ©

SUIT YOURSELF

It is possible to get a tailor-made suit in Bangkok that will wear well in New York and London, but don't jump into the changing room with just any needle pusher. Finding a good tailor is an involved courtship that requires sartorial savvy. Also be aware that Bangkok's tailors are a conservative lot, more adept at the pinstripe banker look than skin-tight playboy.

> First, check out the suit racks back home to determine quality and costs.
> Commission a few small items (shirts, pants) before returning for a high-priced suit.
> For a suit that will last a lifetime, pick a quality imported fabric from a tailor you trust.
> Insist on at least two fittings and be firm when asking for modifications; even the best tailors will send you home if you don't speak up about imperfections.

JASPAL *Fashion*
2nd fl, Emporium, Th Sukhumvit;
10am-10pm; Phrom Phong;
Snag some cute basics from this homegrown alternative to the Gap. Also at Siam Center (p86).

JIM THOMPSON *Fashion*
4th fl, Emporium, Th Sukhumvit;
10am-10pm; Phrom Phong;
Another outlet of the Thai silk company that carries more contemporary fashions. Also at Siam Paragon (p86) and on Th Surawong (p98).

KINOKUNIYA BOOKS *Books*
☎ 0 2664 8554; 3rd fl, Emporium, Th Sukhumvit; 10am-10pm; Phrom Phong;
A smaller version of the Siam Paragon anchor (p83), this branch has a sizeable collection of magazines and children's books.

NANDAKWANG *Handicrafts*
☎ 0 2258 1962; www.nandakwang.com; 108/2-3 Soi 23, Th Sukhumvit; 9am-5pm Mon-Sat, 10am-5pm Sun; Asok, Sukhumvit;
A Chiang Mai–based outfit, Nandakwang's products are utterly cute without being cheesy. From woven drink coasters to embroidered stuffed animals and rugged leather-bottomed satchels, these gifts whisper Thailand without screaming second-rate. There's another branch located on the 4th floor of the Siam Discovery Center (p86).

NICKERMANN'S TAILORS *Tailor*
☎ 0 2252 6682; www.nickermanns. net; basement, Landmark Hotel, 138 Th Sukhumvit; 10am-8.30pm Mon-Sat, noon-6pm Sun; Nana;
Corporate ladies rave about Nickermann's tailor-made power suits: pants and jackets that suit curves

and busts. Formal ball gowns are another area of expertise.

🏛 PHU FA *Handicrafts*
☎ 0 2650 3311; cnr Th Sukhumvit & Soi 7; ⏲ 10am-8pm Mon-Fri, to 6pm Sat & Sun; 🚇 Nana

Gifts with a cause make that fuzzy feeling fuzzier. This outlet sells products from HRH Princess Sirindhorn's economic development program for rural villagers. The Thai-made products are mainly kid-friendly: notebooks, change purses and handwoven Karen textiles.

🏛 PROPAGANDA *Homewares*
4th fl, Emporium, Th Sukhumvit; ⏲ 10am-10pm; 🚇 Phrom Phong; ♿
Housewares and design pieces with an attitude and by local designers can be found at this shop. Also at Siam Discovery Center (p86).

🏛 RAJA'S FASHIONS *Tailor*
☎ 0 2253 8379; 1/6 Soi 4, Th Sukhumvit; ⏲ 10.30am-8.30pm Mon-Sat; 🚇 Nana; ♿

Raja's thrives on a top-notch reputation for men's tailoring (it seems to have besuited Bangkok's entire US-expat population). Just wait for the final fitting when Raja will tell you, like every one of your predecessors, 'You came in good looking and now you're looking good.' Why change a winning formula?

🏛 VILLA MARKET *Groceries*
☎ 0 2662 1000; www.villamarket.com; Soi 33/1, Th Sukhumvit; ⏲ 24hr; 🚇 Phrom Phong
This branch of Bangkok's most well-stocked international grocery store is the place to pick up necessities such as Cheerios and Vegemite. Don't feel wrongfully incriminated if the staff eye your every move – it's simply the Thai concept of 'service'.

EAT
If you choose wisely, you can eat fabulously along this leggy street. A veritable UN of restaurants caters to compatriots and cultured Thais with diplomatic success.

PRETTY THAI FOR A WHITE GUY
Beginning in 2009, a handful of foreigners began opening Thai restaurants in Bangkok. The Thais can be very, well, protective about their cuisine, and the chefs involved generated a huge amount of press – not all of it positive (one Thai food critic accused a well-known foreign restaurateur of 'slapping the faces of Thai people'). The storm has since passed and in its wake we, the unbiased, reap the benefit of several excellent Thai restaurants, including **nahm** (p111), **Sra Bua** (p89), **Bo.lan** (p125) and **Soul Food Mahanakorn** (p129).

Take it lying down at Bed Superclub

MICK ELMORE / LONELY PLANET IMAGES ©

🍴 BED SUPPERCLUB
International $$$
☎ 0 2651 3537; www.bedsupperclub.com; 26 Soi 11, Th Sukhumvit; 🕑 dining 7.30-10pm Tue-Thu, to 9pm Fri & Sat; 🚇 Nana

Within this sleek and futuristic setting – beds instead of tables and contemporary performances instead of mood music – the food stands up to the distractions with a changing menu described as 'modern eclectic cuisine'. Reservations are essential.

🍴 BEI OTTO *German* $$$
☎ 0 2262 0892; www.beiotto.com; 1 Soi 20, Th Sukhumvit; 🕑 9am-midnight; 🚇 Asok, 🚇 Sukhumvit; ♿

Claiming a Bangkok residence for nearly 20 years, Bei Otto's major culinary bragging point is its pork knuckles, reputedly the best in town. A good selection of German beers and an attached delicatessen with brilliant breads and super sausages make it even more attractive to go Deutsch.

🍴 BHARANI *Thai* $$
96/14 Soi 23, Th Sukhumvit; 🕑 9am-10pm; 🚇 Asok, 🚇 Sukhumvit

This cosy Thai restaurant dabbles in a bit of everything, from ox-tongue stew to rice fried with shrimp paste, but the real reason to come is for the rich, meaty 'boat noodles' – so called because they used to be sold from boats plying the *khlong* (canals) of Ayuthaya.

🍴 BO.LAN *Thai* $$$
☎ 0 2260 2962; www.bolan.co.th; 42 Soi Rongnarong Phichai Songkhram, Soi 26, Th Sukhumvit; 🕐 6-11pm Tue-Sun; 🚇 Phrom Phong; 🚭 V

Bo and Dylan (Bo.lan, a play on words that also means 'ancient'), former chefs at London's Michelin-starred nahm, have provided Bangkok with a compelling reason to reconsider upscale Thai cuisine. The couple's scholarly approach to Thai cooking takes the form of seasonal set meals featuring dishes you're not likely to find elsewhere.

🍴 BOON TONG KIAT SINGAPORE HAINANESE CHICKEN RICE *Singaporean* $
☎ 0 2390 2508; 440/5 Soi 55 (Thong Lor), Th Sukhumvit; 🕐 10am-10pm; 🚇 Thong Lo & access by taxi

Order a plate of the restaurant's namesake and bear witness to how a dish can be simultaneously simple and profound. And while you're here you'd be daft not to order *rojak,* the spicy/sour fruit 'salad', which here is cheekily called 'Singapore Som Tam'.

🍴 CABBAGES & CONDOMS
Thai $$$
☎ 0 2229 4610; 10 Soi 12, Th Sukhumvit; 🕐 11am-10pm; 🚇 Asok, 🚇 Sukhumvit; 🚭 🍴 V

It isn't the best Thai food in town, but it is the best cause around. Cabbages & Condoms is affiliated with the Population & Community Development Association (PDA), which is a sex-education/AIDS-prevention organisation credited for Thailand's speedy reaction to the AIDS crisis. In addition to meal names that would make an adolescent chuckle, diners get packaged condoms in lieu of after-dinner mints.

WHAT'S YOUR POISON?
The heat might make you gulp down gallons of water during the day, but when it comes to dinnertime toast your meal with spirit. Beer is a tasty complement to Thai food and can cut through the famous chilli sting. Pilsner-style beers are the usual choices: from locally brewed Singha (pronounced 'sing') to Heineken. An ingenious but provincial custom is the addition of ice cubes to glasses of beer in order to keep the beverage cool. For the sophisti-cates, though, wine is the only respectable tableside date, even though it tends to skunk in Bangkok's hellish climate. Wine is best ordered from places that have dedicated cellars and are able to ensure temperature control from port to table.

CRÊPES & CO

French-Moroccan $$$

☎ 0 2653 3990; www.crepes.co.th; 18/1 Soi 12, Th Sukhumvit; ⏰ 9am-midnight Mon-Sat, 8am-midnight Sun; 🚇 Asok, Ⓜ Sukhumvit; 🚼 Ⓥ

Chic without being pretentious, this breezy cafe is yuppie Bangkok's favourite place for a brunch date. Here you'll tuck into delicate, platter-sized crepes stuffed with such delights as smoky bacon and woodsy mushrooms, and there is lots of thick coffee to soothe your Asian exile.

DOSA KING

Indian-Vegetarian $$

☎ 0 2651 1700; www.dosaking.net; 153/7 Soi 11/1, Th Sukhumvit; ⏰ 11am-11pm; 🚇 Nana; 🚼 Ⓥ

You don't have to get all 'dhal-ed' up to dine on tasty Indian food. (Although a spiffy look would put you in league with the sari-wrapped mothers and clubbing teenagers.)

BREAKFAST IS SERVED

Thailand's interpretation of Western-style breakfast is sometimes in name only, but the effort is both filling and amusing. Wake up in the past at the retro **Federal Hotel coffee shop** (Soi 11, Th Sukhumvit; ⏰ 6am-1am; 🚇 Nana), or retreat to a Western gourmet microcosm at **Kuppa** (right) or **Crêpes & Co** (above).

Divine renditions of the southern-Indian speciality, *dosa* (a thin, stuffed crepe), adorn the tables like ancient parchment scrolls.

FACE *Thai, International* $$$

☎ 0 2713 6048; www.facebars.com; 29 Soi 38, Th Sukhumvit; ⏰ 11am-11pm; 🚇 Thong Lo; Ⓥ

Face is essentially three very good restaurants in one: Lan Na Thai does solid upscale Thai, Misaki focuses on the Japanese end of things, while Hazara dabbles in exotic-sounding 'North Indian frontier cuisine' – all served in a series of interconnected, Thai-style wooden buildings.

KUPPA *International* $$$

☎ 0 2663 0450; 39 Soi 16, Th Sukhumvit; ⏰ 10am-10.30pm; 🚇 Asok, Ⓜ Sukhumvit; 🚼 Ⓥ

Kuppa can pull off all the dishes you thought untranslatable: cream sauces, sophisticated desserts and recognisable cuts of meat. Catch it at weekend brunch when affluent 30-somethings get delivered in chauffeured BMWs.

LE BEAULIEU *French* $$$

☎ 0 2204 2004; www.le-beaulieu.com; 50 Soi 19, Th Sukhumvit; ⏰ 11.30am-3pm & 6.30-11pm; 🚇 Asok, Ⓜ Sukhumvit; 🚼 Ⓥ

This tiny service hotel–bound restaurant is considered by many

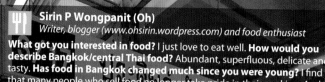

Sirin P Wongpanit (Oh)
Writer, blogger (www.ohsirin.wordpress.com) and food enthusiast

What got you interested in food? I just love to eat well. **How would you describe Bangkok/central Thai food?** Abundant, superfluous, delicate and tasty. **Has food in Bangkok changed much since you were young?** I find that many people who sell food no longer take pride in their cooking. And many eaters today no longer know how to eat. It may be because of today's busy schedules. **Do you have a favourite restaurant?** Rosabieng (p128) is like an oasis in the middle of Bangkok thanks to its surrounding trees. The place serves Thai home-style cooking. **What's your favourite Bangkok market?** For convenience's sake, I always go to Or Tor Kor Market (p139). But things can get very expensive at the fruit and seafood stalls.

residents to be Bangkok's best place for French. The menu ranges from the classic (steak tartare, bouillabaisse) to the modern (*minute* of scrambled eggs and fresh sea urchin), with dishes prepared using both unique imported ingredients and produce from northern Thailand's royally sponsored agriculture projects. Reservations recommended.

🍴 MYEONG GA *Korean* $$$
☎ 0 2229 4658; ground fl, Sukhumvit Plaza, Soi 12, Th Sukhumvit; 🕑 4-11pm; 🚇 Asok, 🚇 Sukhumvit

Located in the multistorey complex colloquially known as Korean Town, Myeong Ga is Bangkok's best destination for authentic 'Seoul' food. If you're with friends, try the Korean barbecue, otherwise the menu spans several tasty one-dish meals as well.

🍴 NASIR AL-MASRI RESTAURANT *Egyptian* $$$
☎ 0 2253 5582; 4/6 Soi 3/1, Th Sukhumvit; 🕑 24hr; 🚇 Nana; 🔗 🔗 Ⓥ

If there was ever a place to wear your sunglasses at night, Nasir Al-Masri is it. With reflective surfaces everywhere, Nasir creates an illusion of oil-money banquets involving artistically arranged sesame-freckled flatbread, creamy hummus and flawlessly fried felafels.

🍴 ROSABIENG RESTAURANT
Thai $$$
☎ 0 2253 5868; 3 Soi 11, Th Sukhumvit; 🕑 11am-11pm; 🚇 Nana

Generous portions of well-prepared central Thai food are served in a leafy garden or in the cool Thai villa. The menu does all the hard work and lays out the recommended dishes for you, but you can't go wrong with the *mèe gròrp* (crispy fried noodle) or the *gaang sôm* (spicy and sour soup with fried acacia and shrimps).

🍴 SOI 38 NIGHT MARKET
Thai-Chinese $
Soi 38, Th Sukhumvit; 🕑 6pm-3am; 🚇 Thong Lo; 🔗

What's a night owl to do when all the bars close up at 2am? Never fear, the good old night market is here. Chow your way to sobriety with a bowl of *bà·mèe mŏo daang* (red pork noodles) or *gŏoay đěeo lòrt* (Chinese-style spring rolls).

🍸 DRINK

🍸 BANGKOK BAR *Bar*
☎ 0 2714 3366; Ekamai Soi 2, Soi 63 (Ekamai), Th Sukhumvit; 🕑 8pm-1am; 🚇 Ekkamai

Bounce with Thai indie kids at this fun but astonishingly uncreatively named bar. There's live music, and the eats are strong enough to make Bangkok Bar a dinner destination in itself. And we double-dog dare you to walk a straight line after two Mad Dogs, the infamous house drink.

☆ BULL'S HEAD *Bar*

☎ 0 2259 4444; 595/10-11 Soi 33/1, Th Sukhumvit; ⏰ 11am-1am; 🚇 Phrom Phong

Bangkok boasts several English-style pubs, and this is probably the most 'authentic' of the lot. With friendly management and staff, and more events and activities than a summer camp, it's also a good place to meet people, particularly those of the British persuasion.

☆ CHEAP CHARLIE'S *Bar*

sub-soi off Soi 11, Th Sukhumvit; ⏰ 5pm-midnight Mon-Sat; 🚇 Nana; ♿

Wild West meets corporate expat at this wooden beer stall, boasting the cheapest brews on Soi 11. Bangkok becomes a road-tested buddy after you down a few bottles of Singha, sweat through your shirt and argue politics with some know-it-all Euro.

☆ IRON FAIRIES *Bar*

www.theironfairies.com; Soi 55 (Thong Lor), Th Sukhumvit; ⏰ 5pm-midnight Mon-Sat; 🚇 Thong Lo & access by taxi

Imagine, if you can, an abandoned fairy factory in Paris c 1912, and

you'll get an idea of the design theme at this very 'in' pub/wine bar. If you manage to wrangle one of a handful of seats, the bar claims to serve Bangkok's best burgers and there's live music after 9.30pm.

☆ SOUL FOOD MAHANAKORN *Bar*

☎ 0 85904 2691; www.soulfoodmaha nakorn.com; 56/10 Soi 55 (Thong Lor), Th Sukhumvit; ⏰ 6.30pm-1am; 🚇 Thong Lo; Ⓥ

Technically a restaurant, Soul Food is a great place to combine the unofficial Thai national pastimes of eating and drinking. Couple one of the tasty house cocktails with regional Thai dishes such as southern-style fried chicken or smoked duck *larb* (a type of northeastern Thai salad).

☆ TITANIUM *Bar*

2/30 Soi 22, Th Sukhumvit; ⏰ 7pm-2am; 🚇 Phrom Phong

Most come to this slightly cheesy 'ice bar' for the chill and flavoured vodka shots, but we come for Unicorn, an all-female rock band.

☆ TUBA *Bar*

34 Room 11-12A, cnr Ekamai Soi 21 & Soi 63 (Ekamai), Th Sukhumvit; ⏰ 7pm-2am; 🚇 Ekkamai & access by taxi

Part storage room for over-the-top vintage furniture, part friendly

See and be seen at popular Q Bar

RICHARD I'ANSON / LONELY PLANET IMAGES ©

local boozer, this bizarre bar certainly doesn't lack in character. Indulge in a whole bottle for once and don't miss the delicious chicken wings.

🍸 WTF *Bar*
www.wtfbangkok.com; 7 Soi 51, Th Sukhumvit; 🕑 6pm–midnight Tue–Sun; 🚇 Thong Lo

No, not that WTF; Wonderful Thai Friendship combines a cosy bar and an art gallery in one attractive package. Top it off with some of Bangkok's best cocktails and some delicious Spanish-influenced bar snacks, and you don't really need another destination for the evening.

130

⭐ PLAY

As a play date for the non-Nana tourist, Sukhumvit is best known for its DJ clubs. Most are located along Soi 55 (Thong Lor) and Soi 63 (Ekamai); see www.thonglor -ekamai.com for reviews of the latest hot spots.

⭐ BED SUPPERCLUB *Dance Club*
☎ 0 2651 3537; www.bedsupperclub. com; 26 Soi 11, Th Sukhumvit; admission from 600B; 🕑 8pm–3am; 🚇 Nana

All white but not virginal, Bed Supperclub complements its fine-dining side with a separate club devoted to resident and international DJs. Famous spinners and hot theme nights keep Bed on clubbers' checklists.

EKAMAI SOI 5 *Dance Club*
cnr Ekamai Soi 5 & Soi 63 (Ekamai), Th Sukhumvit; admission free; 🚇 Ekkamai & access by taxi
This open-air entertainment zone is the destination of choice for Bangkok's young and beautiful – for the moment at least. Demo, with its blasting beats and a NYC warehouse vibe, is the epitome of the Alpha Club, while Funky Villa, with its outdoor seating and Top 40 soundtrack, boasts more of a chill-out vibe. Also accessible via Thong Lor Soi 10.

LIVING ROOM *Live Music*
☎ 0 2264 9888; Sheraton Grande Sukhumvit, 250 Th Sukhumvit; 🕑 6.30pm-midnight; 🚇 Asok, Ⓜ Sukhumvit; &
We'll come clean – the Living Room is a bland hotel lounge. But where most of its ilk are sedated by corny covers bands, this cosy upmarket place is alive with the grooves of some of the top jazz acts around. A mellow, jazz-based Sunday brunch starts at around 11am.

NUNG-LEN *Dance Club*
☎ 0 2711 6564; www.nunglen.net; 217 Soi 63 (Ekamai), Th Sukhumvit; admission free; 🕑 8pm-2am; 🚇 Ekkamai & access by taxi
Young, loud and Thai, Nung-Len (literally 'sit and chill') is a ridiculously popular sardine tin of live music and uni students on popular Soi 63 (Ekamai). Make sure you get in before 10pm or you're not getting in at all.

Q BAR *Dance Club*
☎ 0 2252 3274; www.qbarbangkok.com; 34 Soi 11, Th Sukhumvit; admission from 600B; 🕑 8pm-2am; 🚇 Nana; &
The club that introduced Bangkok to the lounge scene in 1999 is still alive and writhing. This darkened industrial space sees a revolving cast of somebodies, nobodies and working girls. Various theme nights fill the weekly calendar.

SFX CINEMA *Cinema*
☎ 0 2268 8888; 6th fl, Emporium, Th Sukhumvit; 🚇 Phrom Phong; & ⚥
On the top floor of the Emporium shopping centre, this cinema serves up the usual Hollywood shoot-and-snog standards. But this cinema stands out because of its fab sound and projection quality.

>GREATER BANGKOK

Outside central Bangkok, the neighbourhoods become more Thai and more suburban, meaning that fewer commercial signs are in roman script and the roads become highways and flyovers. One concentration of community can be found near Victory Monument, a large traffic circle pinned by a memorial to an obscure Siamese victory over the French. In the shadow of the Victory Monument BTS station is a night market that feeds and clothes many Thai students who live nearby. The elevated walkway that nearly circumnavigates the roundabout is treated like a university quad for catwalking youth fashions.

The last stop on the northern extension of the BTS line is the mother of all markets: Chatuchak Weekend Market, the sole reason most tourists venture beyond the city centre. Across the street you'll find fruit and veg galore at Or Tor Kor Market. Another suburban draw is RCA (Royal City Avenue), a strip mall of nightclubs currently dominating the city's social calendar.

GREATER BANGKOK

⊙ SEE
Baiyoke Tower 1 C5
Bangkok Doll Factory
 & Museum 2 D5
Children's Discovery
 Museum 3 D2
Suan Phakkad Palace
 Museum 4 C5
Victory Monument 5 C5

🏃 DO
Blue Elephant Thai
 Cooking School 6 B7
House of Dhamma 7 E2
Royal Turf Club 8 B5

🏠 SHOP
Chatuchak Weekend
 Market 9 D2
Talat Rot Fai 10 D2

🍽 EAT
Mallika 11 C5
Or Tor Kor Market 12 D3
Pathé 13 E2
River Bar Café 14 A3

🍸 DRINK
Tawandang German
 Brewery 15 D8

Th Kamphaeng Phet
 Bars 16 D3

⭐ PLAY
808 Club ....(see 20)
Aksra Theatre 17 C5
Cosmic Café ....(see 20)
Flix/Slim ....(see 20)
House ....(see 20)
Mansion 7 ....18 E4
Raintree Pub 19 C5
RCA 20 F5
Route 66 ....(see 20)
Saxophone Pub &
 Restaurant 21 C5
Zeta ....(see 20)

Please see over for map

◉ SEE

◉ BAIYOKE TOWER

☎ 0 2656 3456; 222 Th Ratchaprarop; admission incl access to 77th, 83rd & 84th fl 220-250B; ⏱ 10am-10pm; ⊠ Phaya Thai or Ratchaprarop, 🚌 17, 73, 504, 514; ♿

It's a bird; it's a crane; no, it's the Baiyoke Tower, the nation's tallest scraper, measuring a gangly 88 storeys (309m tall). On the 84th floor is a revolving observation deck, something akin to a geriatric carnival ride. This is the only sky-high perch in Bangkok geared towards families.

◉ BANGKOK DOLL FACTORY & MUSEUM

☎ 0 2245 3008; 85 Soi Ratchataphan, Th Ratchaprarop; admission free; ⏱ 8am-5pm Mon-Sat; ⊠ Victory Monument & access by taxi; ♿

New and antique dolls dressed in national costumes are displayed for appreciation, while the gift shop sells on-site factory–made dolls, a unique industry that helped preserve Thai traditional costumes in miniature. The museum is difficult to find; the best approach is from Th Sri Ayuthaya heading east.

◉ CHILDREN'S DISCOVERY MUSEUM

☎ 0 2615 7333; Queen Sirikit Park, Th Kamphaeng Phet 4; admission 70/50B; ⏱ 9am-5pm Tue-Fri, 10am-6pm Sat & Sun; ⊠ Mo Chit, ◉ Chatuchak Park & access by taxi; ♿

Through hands-on activities, learning is well disguised as fun. Kids can stand inside a bubble or see how an engine works. Most activities are geared towards children aged between five and 10 years. There is also a toddler-suitable playground at the back of the main building. You'll find the museum opposite Chatuchak Weekend Market.

WORTH THE TRIP

Claiming to be the largest open-air museum in the world, **Ancient City** (Muang Boran; ☎ 0 2709 1644; www.ancientcity.com; 296/1 Th Sukhumvit, Samut Prakan; admission 400/200B; ⏱ 8am-5pm Tue-Sun by appointment; 🚌 511) covers more than 80 hectares of peaceful countryside littered with 109 scaled-down facsimiles of many of the kingdom's most famous monuments. It's an excellent place to explore by bicycle (daily rental 50B), as it is usually quiet and never crowded. Ancient City lies outside Samut Prakan, which is accessible via air-con bus 511 from the east end of Th Sukhumvit. Upon reaching the bus terminal at Pak Nam, board minibus 36, which passes the entrance to Ancient City.

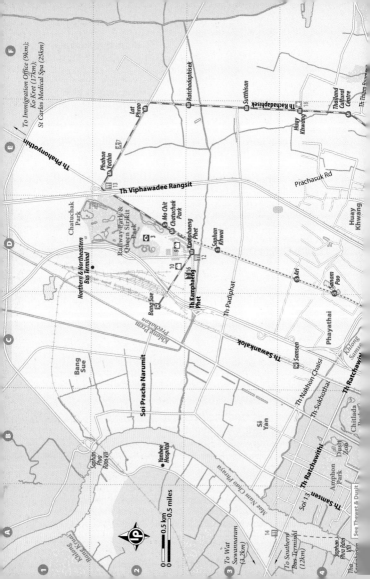

🔵 SUAN PHAKKAD PALACE MUSEUM

☎ 0 2245 4934; Th Sri Ayuthaya; admission 100B; 🕓 9am-4pm; 🚇 Phaya Thai

Of Bangkok's traditional house museums, Suan Phakkad is a nice counterpoint to Jim Thompson's house. The displays are less formal, allowing enough room to wander and wonder. There are eight traditional wooden houses filled with Thai art and knick-knacks, including pottery from Bronze Age Ban Chiang, masks from the *khon* dance-drama and traditional musical instruments. The most famous exhibit is the Lacquer Pavilion, which was moved here from a monastery near Ayuthaya and is decorated with intricate gold-leaf and black-lacquer *Jataka* (stories of the Buddha) and *Ramakian* (Thailand's version of India's *Ramayana)* murals. The palace grounds were once a farm and, later, the home of Princess Chumbon of Nakhon Sawan.

🔵 VICTORY MONUMENT

Th Ratchawithi & Th Phayathai;
🚇 **Victory Monument**

A busy traffic circle revolves around this obelisk that commemorates a 1939 Thai victory against the French in Laos. An elevated walkway circumnavigates the roundabout, funnelling the pedestrian traffic in and out of the

Impress friends back home after a class at Blue Elephant Thai Cooking School   GREG ELMS / LONELY PLANET IMAGES ©

WORTH THE TRIP

Looking for a day at the races? Horse racing is alive and well in the kingdom and brings out the same frenzied energy of gambling and drinking as it does elsewhere. The public seats are right beside the finish line and horses kick up mud and sweat as they thunder past. English-language schedules are around and unhelpful betting tips handed out by every bystander. The races are held on weekends, either at the **Royal Bangkok Sports Club** (Map p79, C3; ☎ 0 2652 5000; 1 Th Henri Dunant; 🕐 12.30-6pm; 🚇 Ratchadamri), which hosts every other Saturday or Sunday, or the **Royal Turf Club** (☎ 0 2628 1810; 183 Th Phitsanulok; 🕐 12.30-6pm; 🚌 509), which hosts the alternate Sundays. The Royal Turf Club also hosts Bangkok's biggest horse race, the King's Cup, around the first or second week of January.

BTS station as well as providing a gathering spot for break-dancers, flirting gangs of guys and gals, and lots of fashion experiments. Because Victory Monument is outside the core of Bangkok, the neighbourhood is less cosmopolitan and more reminiscent of provincial towns elsewhere in the country.

DO

🏃 BLUE ELEPHANT THAI COOKING SCHOOL *Cooking School*
☎ 0 2673 9353; www.blueelephant. com; 233 Th Sathon Tai; classes 2943B; 🕐 8.45am-1pm & 1.15-4.30pm Mon-Sat; 🚇 Surasak
Devotees of Julia Child will enjoy the culinary professionalism of this restaurant-associated school. Both sessions get a main course of Thai cooking theory and hands-on meal preparation of four courses.

Morning classes include a market tour.

🏃 HOUSE OF DHAMMA
Meditation
☎ 0 2511 0439; www.houseofdhamma. com; 26/9 Soi 15, Th Lat Phrao; donations accepted; 🚇 Lat Phrao
Helen Jandamit has opened her suburban Bangkok home to meditation retreats and classes in *vipassana* (insight meditation). Check the website to see what workshops are on offer, and be sure to call ahead before making a visit.

🏃 MANOHRA CRUISES
Cooking School
☎ 0 2476 0022; Bangkok Marriott Resort & Spa, Th Charoen Nakhorn; minimum 4 people 2800B; 🕐 8am-noon; 🚤 free shuttle boat from Tha Sathon
Here's a novel idea – whip up a curry while you're cruising the

river at the same time. Classes arranged through Manohra Cruises include a market tour as well as a cooking lesson aboard a restored rice barge boat. Now that's a mouthful.

SHOP
CHATUCHAK WEEKEND MARKET *Market*
☎ 0 2272 4440; bounded by Th Kamphaeng Phet, Chatuchak Park & Th Phahonyothin; ⏰ 8am-6pm Sat & Sun; 🚇 Mo Chit, 🚈 Chatuchak Park

You've got to see it to believe it: this weekend market is a veritable village of vendor stalls selling clothes, homewares, junk as well as collectables. It is the number-one shopping destination in the city despite the heat and crowds. For more information, see p24.

🚉 TALAT ROT FAI *Market*
Th Kamphaeng Phet; ⏰ 5pm-midnight Sat & Sun; 🚈 Kamphaeng Phet

Set in a sprawling abandoned rail yard, this market is all about the retro, from antique enamel platters to secondhand Vespas. With mobile snack vendors, VW van–based bars and even a few land-bound pubs, it's more than just a shopping destination.

🍴 EAT
🍴 MALLIKA *Thai* $$
☎ 0 2248 0287; 21/36 Th Rang Nam; ⏰ 10am-10pm Mon-Sat; 🚉 Victory Monument; ♿ 🚻

WORTH THE TRIP

Soothe your nerves with a half-day getaway to **Ko Kret**, a car-free island in the middle of Mae Nam Chao Phraya, at Bangkok's northern edge. Actually an artificial island, the result of dredging a canal in a sharp bend in the river, the island is home to one of Thailand's oldest settlements of Mon people, who were the dominant culture in central Thailand between the 6th and 10th centuries AD. The Mon are also skilled potters, and Ko Kret continues the culture's ancient tradition of hand-thrown earthenware, made from local Ko Kret clay.

If you come on a weekday you'll likely have the entire island to yourself. There are a couple of temples worth peeking into and a few places to eat, but the real highlight is taking in the bucolic riverside atmosphere. On weekends things change drastically and Ko Kret is an extremely popular destination for urban Thais. There's heaps more food, drink and things for sale, but with this come the crowds.

To get here, take a taxi from Mo Chit or Chatuchak Park stations, or bus 32 from Th Maha Rat to Pak Kret, before boarding the cross-river ferry that leaves from Wat Sanam Neua.

7-ELEVEN FOREVER

According to the company's website there are 3912 branches of 7-Eleven in Thailand alone (there will inevitably be several more by the time this book has gone to print) – more than half the number found in the entire USA. In Bangkok, 7-Elevens are so ubiquitous that it's not uncommon to see two branches staring at each other from across the street.

The first *sewên* (as it's known in Thai) in Thailand was installed in Patpong in 1991. The brand caught on almost immediately, and today Thailand ranks behind only Japan and Taiwan in the total number of branches in Asia.

Although the company claims that its stores carry more than 2000 items, the fresh flavours of Thai cuisine are not reflected in the wares of a typical Bangkok 7-Eleven, whose food selections are even junkier than those of its counterparts in the West. Like all shops in Thailand, alcohol is only available from 11am to 2pm and 5pm to 11pm, and branches of 7-Eleven located near hospitals, temples and schools do not sell alcohol or cigarettes at all (but do continue to sell unhealthy snack food).

Fans of spice will adore this outpost of authentic southern Thai–style cooking. If you're looking for a buzz, try the incendiary *kôoa glîng* (pork or beef stir-fried in a southern-style chilli paste). For the rest of us, there's an expansive English-language menu, good service and a tidy setting.

🍴 OR TOR KOR MARKET *Thai* $
Th Kamphaeng Phet; 🕐 **10am-5pm;** 🚇 **Kamphaeng Phet;** ♿
Across the street from Chatuchak Weekend Market, the 'Marketing Organisation for Farmers' market is Bangkok's most upscale, selling what many swear are the tastiest pomelos around. Next to the produce vendors are food stalls that earn equal veneration for duck curries and other street treats.

🍴 PATHÉ *Thai* $$
☎ **0 2938 4995; cnr Th Lad Phrao & Th Viphawadee Rangsit;** 🕐 **2pm-1am;** 🚇 **Phahon Yothin**
Bangkok's answer to the 1950s-era American diner, this popular place combines solid eats, a fun atmosphere and a jukebox that plays scratched records. Try any of the numerous Thai dishes, many twisted just slightly as to make them 'new', and don't miss the delicious deep-fried ice cream.

🍴 RIVER BAR CAFÉ *Thai* $$
☎ **0 2879 1747; www.riverbar.com; 450/1 Soi Chao Phraya, Th Ratchawithi;** 🕐 **5pm-midnight;** 🚤 **taxi**
This open-air restaurant-bar combines all of the essentials of a perfect Bangkok night out: a

 Gene Kasidit
Rock 'n' Roller

Western or Thai music? Either. It depends on the mood I'm in, really. As long as I can avoid the super cheesy tunes of both cultures, then I'm fine. **How would you describe Thai pop music?** Very melodic and often too cheesy at times, but I guess that's its charm. **What local bands do you like?** I love Moderndog, Ornaree, Slur, The Jukks, Lomosonic and many others. **Where's a good place in Bangkok for live music?** I like Cosmic Café (p142). It usually has decent rock bands on the weekends, and occasionally some electronic bands. **How would you describe your own music?** Electric black diamond heart on high heels. **Your influences?** Sex, ducks, rock 'n' roll and life, as it is.

picture-perfect riverside location, good food and live music. For a truly Bangkok drinking snack, sample the grilled squid sold from boats that float by.

 DRINK

TAWANDANG GERMAN BREWERY *Bar*

☎ 0 2678 1119; www.tawandang.com; cnr Th Phra Ram III & Th Narathiwat Ratchanakharin; ⏰ 5pm-1am; 🚇 Chong Nonsi & access by taxi; ♿

Seeking a more local feel than your average expat bar? You asked for it – Tawandang is a massive beer hall and German-style microbrewery *(rohng beea)*. Between sets of singalong pop tunes, choruses of 'Happy Birthday' erupt from the overcrowded tables.

TH KAMPHAENG PHET BARS *Bar*

Th Kamphaeng Phet; ⏰ 6pm-2.30am; 🚇 Kamphaeng Phet

For something a little different, intrepid partiers haul themselves out to the mainly Thai scene located near Chatuchak. Fake Club and el Ninyo set the pink theme that dominates much of the area, while the hyper-hetero rock vibe at Hot Rock confirms that there's a bit of something for everybody here.

 PLAY

AKSRA THEATRE *Theatre*

☎ 0 2677 8888, ext 5730; www.aksra theatre.com; 3rd fl, King Power Complex, 8/1 Th Rang Nam; tickets 400-600B; ⏰ shows 7.30-8.30pm Mon-Wed, dinner shows 6.30-7pm Thu-Sun; 🚇 Victory Monument; ♿

A variety of performances are now held at this modern theatre, but the highlight are performances of the *Ramakian* with knee-high puppets that require three puppeteers to strike humanlike poses. Come early in the week for a performance in the Aksra Theatre, or later for Thai buffet coupled with a show in the theatre's dining room.

MANSION 7 *Shopping Centre*

☎ 0 2476 0022; www.themansion7. com; cnr Soi 14 & Th Rachadaphisek; ⏰ noon-midnight; Ⓜ Huay Khwang

It was a struggle to find an appropriate category for this self-professed 'Boutique Thriller Mall', but the combination of Food (there's a handful of restaurants and bars), Fashion (several boutiques and a nail salon) and Fear (there's a haunted house) landed it here. Great for a quirky, scary night out.

RAINTREE PUB *Bar, Live Music*

☎ 0 2245 7230; 116/63-64 Th Rang Nam; ⏰ 6pm-1am; 🚇 Victory Monument

Decorated like a country-and-western bar with driftwood and

buffalo horns, Raintree is a relic in Bangkok's music scene. The nightly bands carry on the 'songs for life' tradition, one of Thailand's most unique adaptations of rock music, that has now passed from current to classic.

⭐ RCA *Dance Club*
Royal City Ave, Th Phra Ram IX; admission free; ☽ 9pm-2am; ☻ Phra Ram 9 & access by taxi

After more than a decade, Royal City Avenue, a somewhat inconveniently located strip of clubs, continues to be the to-go destination for go go–free late-night fun in Bangkok. **808 Club** (www.808bangkok. com; admission from 600B) is currently the leader of the pack with bigname DJs and insanely crowded events. If the joint isn't jumping then check out the surrounding clubs, such as **Flix/Slim** (admission free), **Route 66** (www.route66club.com; admission free) or the low-key **Cosmic Café** (admission free).

⭐ SAXOPHONE PUB & RESTAURANT *Live Music*
☎ 0 2246 5472; www.saxophonepub. com; 3/8 Th Phayathai, Victory Monument; ☽ 6pm-2am; ☻ Victory Monument; ♿

Saxophone is still Bangkok's premier live-music venue, a dark, intimate space where you can pull up a chair just a few metres away from the band and see their every bead of sweat. If you like some mystique in your musicians, watch the blues, jazz, reggae or rock from the balcony.

⭐ ZETA *Gay & Lesbian*
☎ 0 2203 0994; 29/67 Block S, Royal City Avenue, Th Phra Ram IX; admission 100B; ☽ 8pm-2am Tue-Sat; ☻ Phra Ram 9 & access by taxi

All of Bangkok's *tom-dees* (lesbians) complain that there is no dedicated space for girls who love girls. But Zeta has come to the rescue, offering an upscale RCA club dedicated to the ladies, including an all-female staff.

>EXCURSIONS

CHRIS MELLOR / LONELY PLANET IMAGES ©
Traditional trading at Damnoen Saduak (p148) floating market

AYUTHAYA

Designated a Unesco World Heritage Site, the temple ruins of Ayuthaya are all that remain of the former capital's illustrious heyday. Before Bangkok rose up from the river basin to become the behemoth city it is today, the Siamese capital sat 85km north of the modern one along the mighty Mae Nam Chao Phraya and enjoyed patronage from the roving sea merchants of the Asian trade route.

The Siamese royal capital flourished from 1350 to 1767 and was named after Ayodhya, the Sanskrit word for 'unassailable' or 'undefeatable', as well as the home of Rama in the Indian epic *Ramayana*. An auspicious name didn't prevail against the eventual Burmese sacking in 1767 that ended the island city's reign. The invading army looted the city's golden treasures and carted off the royal family as prisoners. The nervous system of the emerging Thai nation fractured into competing factions until General Taksin united the territories and established a new capital near Bangkok a mere three years later. The Burmese eventually abandoned their Thai conquest.

Ayuthaya then developed into a provincial trading town while its once-magnificent monuments succumbed to gravity and looters. More than 400 temples were built in the ancient city, now the centre of the modern town. Some of the surviving temples have been restored but very few Buddha images remain intact, due to inoperable war wounds. Today, cultural tourists scoot about on bicycles or motorcycles photographing the historical survivors.

Nature sculpted the most famous attraction at **Wat Phra Mahathat** – a sandstone Buddha head embedded in twisted tree roots. The sacred image is doubly auspicious because of the tree's embrace, a physical combination of formal Buddhism and folk animism.

INFORMATION

Information Ayuthaya Tourist Office (☎ 0 3524 6076/7; 108/22 Th Si Sanphet; ⏰ 9am-5pm).

Getting there Train from Bangkok's Hualamphong station (15B to 66B, 1½ hours, every hour from 4.20am to 11.40pm); bus from Bangkok's Northern & Northeastern bus terminal (56B, 1½ hours, frequent departures).

Getting around Guesthouses on Soi 1, Th Naresuan, rent bicycles and motorbikes. Informal boat tours (from 200B per hour) can be arranged at river piers.

Explore Khmer-style ruins at Wat Chai Wattanaram

OLIVER STREWE / LONELY PLANET IMAGES ©

Wat Ratburana retains one of the best-preserved Khmer-style *prang* (towers) in old Ayuthaya. It was built in the 15th century by King Borom Rachathirat II in honour of his two brothers, who died battling each other for the throne. **Wat Phra Si Sanphet**, the biggest temple of its time, has three surviving stupas in the classic bell-shaped, Ayuthaya style. Built in the late 14th century, the compound was used for important royal ceremonies and once contained a 16m-high standing Buddha (Phra Si Sanphet) covered with 250kg of gold.

In the evenings, many ruin-hoppers take a semicircle **boat ride** (arranged at local guesthouses) around the island, with stops at **Wat Phanan Choeng**, a popular pilgrimage destination for Thai-Chinese who come to honour the Chinese explorer Sam Po Kong (Zheng He), who visited the capital in 1407.

Shutterbugs will want to visit **Wat Chai Wattanaram** in time for sunset to catch the silhouette of the Khmer-style *prang* alongside the river. Extensively restored, the temple was built in the 17th century by King Prasat Thong in honour of his mother.

The remainder of the boat ride winds through the riverside communities, where meals are cooked, dishes are washed and TV commercials echo from the banks. The trip ends at the night market, a fixture in the daily life of a typical Thai town, despite its ancient pedigree.

EXCURSIONS

KO SAMET

Bangkok's beachside playground is a T-bone-shaped island of squeaky blond beaches, glassy water and not a single high-rise – surprisingly rustic considering its proximity to the capital. That doesn't mean this is castaway paradise, though; Ko Samet sits solidly on the beaten track with weekend crowds, jet skis, discos, sarong-sellers and beach masseuses. But footpaths skirting the rocky exterior provide mental, if not physical, seclusion.

Before being designated a national park in 1981, Ko Samet claimed literary distinction thanks to Thai poet Sunthorn Phu's epic *Phra Aphaimani*. In this classical poem, a prince was exiled to an undersea kingdom from which a mermaid helped him escape to Ko Samet. This scene is memorialised on the island with a weatherworn statue of the two built on a rocky point that separates the sights of Ao Hin Khok and Hat Sai Kaew.

Most boats from the mainland arrive at Na Dan pier, Samet's 'commercial' area filled with a short block of shophouses and rutted roads. A short walk west leads you to **Hat Sai Kaew** (Diamond Beach), the longest and most populous of Ko Samet's beaches. Tucked behind the treeline are moderately priced and average beachside guesthouses. Around the next headland are scruffy **Ao Hin Khok** and **Ao Phai**, two small bays fittingly claimed by backpackers and bars. Ao Phai is beginning a steady image upgrade with some of the older guesthouses transforming into more

Needing time out from the big city? Take respite on palm-fringed Hat Sai Kaew   RICHARD NEBESKY / LONELY PLANET IMAGES ©

INFORMATION

Location Ko Samet is 200km southeast of Bangkok and accessible by public bus to the port town of Ban Phe, where boats depart for the island. There is a 200/100B national-park entrance fee.

Getting there Bus from Bangkok's Ekkamai station directly to Ban Phe (167B, three hours, every 30 minutes), then take the ferry to Ko Samet (100/50B, 45 minutes, hourly).

Accommodation Samed Villa (☎ 0 3864 4094; www.samedvilla.com; Ao Phai; bungalows 1800-5000B) and Sametville Resort (☎ 0 3865 1681/2; www.sametvilleresort.com; Ao Wai; bungalows 1380-6280B).

stylish models. Next in line is **Ao Phutsa**, a nice little curve of sand before a lengthy run of rocky headlands leading to **Ao Wong Deuan**, a beach that resembles the girlie-bar scene of Pattaya, and **Ao Thian** (Candlelight Beach), claimed by Thai college kids and all-night guitar jams. The southern bays of **Ao Wai** and **Ao Kiu Na Nok** are deliciously secluded. Armed with enough water and sunscreen you can follow the oceanfront footpaths as far south as your feet and your stomach will take you.

On the northeastern shores is **Ao Phrao**, dubbed Paradise Beach in English and claimed by two top-end beach resorts and surrounding sea breezes. The resorts' waterfront bars are popular pilgrimages for sunset-watchers and the affiliated spa offers all of the mainland relaxation treatments.

And what should you do amid these jewel-toned waters? Be warned that a beach blanket and book are an invitation for the itinerant merchants to approach multiple times selling massages, sarongs and henna tattoos. A simple 'no thank you' minus a smile is culturally polite and doesn't invite badgering. Beyond sunning and splashing, boat tours head out to coral-filled snorkelling spots, secluded islands and the Turtle Conservation Centre on nearby **Ko Man Nai**. Dive operators shuttle out to the underwater rock formations of **Hin Pholeung**, a bit of a trek from Samet.

When your workout is done, you can nibble at freshly caught fish at one of the many beachside barbecues. Then meet and swill with other visitors at the open-air bars that specialise in Red Bull and vodka buckets, a Thai beach concoction.

On weekends and holidays, almost all of Bangkok flocks to Samet's shores, making it difficult to find accommodation upon arrival. More and more, businesses on Samet are copying the big-city convention of using and honouring reservations, a necessity in peak periods.

EXCURSIONS

FLOATING MARKETS

In olden times, central Thai farmers would deliver their goods to market aboard the only transport they owned: the family boat. This tradition has been widely photographed – slim dugout canoes loaded with brightly coloured fruits and vegetables sidling up to a riverbank dock – but this iconic image is more historical than current. The floating markets that once dotted the canals have been replaced with terrestrial markets and the boats with motorcycles thanks to the advancement of asphalt and cars.

The most famous survivor is **Damnoen Saduak**, which appears on every package-tour itinerary. Once one of the largest floating markets in the area, attracting vendors from near and far, today Damnoen Saduak sells more trinkets than bananas. Many tourists are disappointed not to find the old ways in action, but there are some redeeming qualities should you be committed to a visit. Slender longtail boats are the mode of exploration, with a requisite stop for a bowl of 'boat noodles', prepared by a canoe cook. Then the real souvenir blitz begins – if you haven't already loaded up on wooden knick-knacks, you're in luck.

Beyond the market stalls is further evidence of the riverside life of central Thais: houses built on stilts along the water's edge and small floating gas stations filling up longtail boats.

CRAIG PERSHOUSE / LONELY PLANET IMAGES ©
Take your pick at Damnoen Saduak floating market

Across the river from Bangkok in Thonburi is the floating food market of **Taling Chan**. Several docks on Khlong Bangkok Yai carry on the old tradition of floating meals. On either side of the docks are longtail boats outfitted with portable kitchens: charcoal grills for toasting gulf shrimp or whole fish, while other boats balance steaming pots of soup. Diners kick off their shoes and shimmy up to the low tables for a complicated family meal or a quick nibble before picking up fruits and sundries from the roadside vendors.

When Thais feel like reliving the days of yore, they go to **Talat Ban Mai**, an atmospheric riverside

---

INFORMATION

Damnoen Saduak
Location Damnoen Saduak is 70km southwest of Bangkok and is open from 6am to noon, Saturday and Sunday.
Getting there Bus from Thonburi's Southern bus terminal (80B, two hours, every 20 minutes from 6am to 9pm).
Getting around Longtail-boat hire at Damnoen Saduak (per hour 300B).

Taling Chan
Location Taling Chan is 15km west of Bangkok in Thonburi and is open from 9am to 3pm, Saturday and Sunday.
Getting there City bus 79 or 83 from Th Ratchadamnoen Klang or Ratchaprasong (16B, 25 minutes, frequent).

Talat Ban Mai
Location Talat Ban Mai is in Chachoengsao, 80km east of Bangkok, and is open from 7am to 7pm, Saturday and Sunday.
Getting there Bus from Bangkok's Ekkamai bus station (90B, 1½ hours, frequent departures), or train from Hualamphong station (13B to 57B, two hours, roughly hourly departures) to Chachoengsao.

---

market that originated 100 years ago. Today the old-fashioned wooden shophouses teetering on the riverbank are mainly a weekend attraction for local Thais prowling for good eats. Many businesses are owned by the second and third generation of ethnic Teochew Chinese who migrated to Thailand's central plains in search of work. The story of these immigrants is a classic success tale; many arrived with only a suitcase and a few coins in their pocket, labouring on farms and in factories with enough diligence to secure a merchant future for their children and a university education for their grandchildren. The market's Chinese heritage continues with the foods on offer – *gǒoay chái* (dumplings stuffed with green veg) and *galorchi* (sweet, deep-fried tapioca patties).

A visit here contains all the components for a true Thai outing – food, trinkets, a temple visit, more food. You can combine a trip to the market with a **boat tour** (☎ 0 3851 4333; tours 100B; ☼ hourly 9am-3pm Sat & Sun) along Mae Nam Bang Pakong, beginning at Wat Sothon Wararam Worawihan in Chachoengsao town. From November to February, this brackish river is full of striped catfish that entice hungry dolphins in from the Gulf of Thailand.

Art and temples or food and drink? Shopping or meditation? Traditional Thai massage or a kelp body wrap? In Bangkok, you really don't have to choose one over the other, but you might need a bit of background information and perhaps some pointing in the right direction.

GREG ELMS / LONELY PLANET IMAGES

Cross paths with everyone and everything on the streets of Banglamphu (p50)

> ACCOMMODATION

Bangkok has always known how to look after its visitors. In the days of steamer travel, the Oriental Hotel was the home-away-from-home for adventurous artists and writers, such as William Somerset Maugham, who spent months there recovering from a bout of malaria. During and after the Vietnam War, American soldiers spent R&R time in hotels named after cities back home, such as Reno and Miami, while travellers on the overland hippy trail crashed at guesthouses around Soi Ngam Duphli. These days, visitors are more likely to hit the sack in the famous backpackers' ghetto of Th Khao San or live it up on a package holiday to luxury riverside hotels.

Hotels in Bangkok cover the gamut with all the attendant global trends. Most top-enders are international chains. Amenities, standards and views are phenomenal at these spots, and rates are relatively affordable compared with other metropolitan destinations worldwide. The latest trend in the upper budget range is the emergence of intimate inns that are reclaiming the old parts of the city where warehouses once slumbered.

The midrange options vary from superb to disturbed. Some are great value with fewer amenities than the big-budget hotels but with ideal locations, while others betray Bangkok's Third World reputation. Beds might be a little dodgy and service a little rough around the edges.

Call us unrepentant backpackers, but Bangkok still has the best selection of budget digs around. And the quality keeps getting better as prices climb nominally. More and more dive hotels are being spruced up to include en suites, air-con and fresh coats of paint, making a little baht go a lot further.

You've got your budget figured out, now you need to pick a neighbourhood. Most neighbourhoods are segregated into budget ranges:

ie cheap guesthouses flock together in Banglamphu, while luxury hotels claim waterfront locations in the Riverside area. Another consideration is mobility. Getting around Bangkok can be a challenge, so you'll want to sleep and play in the same neighbourhood or near public transport.

Business travellers tend to stay in the white-collar districts of Silom and Sukhumvit, districts also favoured by lone male travellers for their proximity to 'entertainment' areas such as Patpong, Nana Entertainment Plaza and Soi Cowboy. Although many package deals are available for hotels in Silom and the lower-numbered *soi* (lanes) of Th Sukhumvit, families or female travellers might prefer to stay in other parts of the city.

The area around Siam Square is convenient for shopaholics and is close to the BTS train line for quick trips to Sukhumvit or Silom. This is one of the most diverse budget areas, with options representing classy and homey.

The most charming place to stay is along the river, in the area referred to as Riverside, or further north in Ko Ratanakosin or Banglamphu. In these neighbourhoods, traffic can thwart an ill-timed outing. Luckily the river express boat provides an escape to many attractions. Riverside is dominated by high-end chains; Ko Ratanakosin is filling up with boutique inns; and Banglamphu is a gentrified backpackers' ghetto. Devoid of pushy tailors or túk-túk drivers, Chinatown has become an 'adventurous' travellers' outpost. However, mobility is difficult due to daytime traffic.

BEST FOR MODERN SOPHISTICATION

> Metropolitan Hotel (www.metropolitan.como.bz)
> Millennium Hilton (www.bangkok.hilton.com)
> Luxx (www.staywithluxx.com)

BEST FOR COOL FACTOR

> Arun Residence (www.arunresidence.com)
> Ma Du Zi (www.maduzihotel.com)
> Siam@Siam (www.siamatsiam.com)

BEST FOR CLASSICAL THAI

> Siam Heritage (www.thesiamheritage.com)
> Chakrabongse Villas (www.thaivillas.com)
> Old Bangkok Inn (www.oldbangkokinn.com)
> AriyasomVilla (www.ariyasom.com)
> Ban Dinso (www.bandinso.com)

BEST VALUE

> Lamphu Tree House (www.lamphutreehotel.com)
> Stable Lodge (www.stablelodge.com)
> Rikka Inn (www.rikkainn.com)
> Baan Saladaeng (www.baansaladaeng.com)

> ARTS & ARCHITECTURE

As the capital of the current dynasty, Bangkok is the nation's artistic repository, cultivating modern artists with royal patronage and preserving the art forms that were reserved solely for the royal courts. In short, Bangkok is the centre of Thailand's formal arts, from temple paintings to dance-dramas. It is also the nexus of contemporary arts, from graffiti to photography.

Bangkok's most impressive examples of traditional painting and sculpture are religious in nature. Temple murals painted in fantastic colours and mythological characters depict instructive sermons based on the life of Buddha or recount the *Ramakian*, the epic story adapted from India's *Ramayana*. Thai sculpture throughout its different artistic periods represents some of the world's leading examples of Buddhist iconography.

Thailand began to adopt modern artistic principles in the 20th century thanks to an Italian artist named Corrado Feroci, who helped establish Silpakorn, the first fine-arts university in the kingdom. Today, Thai creatives

GREG ELMS / LONELY PLANET IMAGES ©

BEST MUSEUMS & GALLERIES
> National Museum (p43)
> Dusit Palace Park (p67)
> Bangkok Art & Culture Centre (p80)
> Museum of Siam (p42)

BEST FOR ARCHITECTURE
> Wat Phra Kaew (p42; pictured above)
> Wat Arun (p44)
> Jim Thompson's House (p80)
> Suan Phakkad Palace Museum (p136)
> Ban Kamthieng (p115)

Delve into Thai art and history at the National Museum (p43)

MICK ELMORE / LONELY PLANET IMAGES ©

continue to capture a distinctively 'Thai' essence in modern painting and photography: religious themes are often explored through modern images, and brilliant colours shape abstract scenes. In the past 10 years, the city has seen a proliferation of private galleries, mainly in the Sukhumvit and Silom areas, showcasing new and established talent.

The dance-drama known as *khon* involves masked dancers depicting scenes from the *Ramakian*. Today, *khon* performances aren't cloistered in the royal courts, but are occasionally performed for the general public at the National Theatre (p48) and Chalermkrung Royal Theatre (p77).

Pottery and decorative arts in Thailand received much tutelage from China, but the enduring traditions of celadon (green-glazed porcelain) and *benjarong* (five-colour porcelain) retain a distinctive interplay of colours and elegance that define the Thai aesthetic. Modern interpretations of pottery and woodwork are enjoying great commercial success, as is haute fashion using Thai silks and colour schemes.

Although modern Bangkok may seem like an architectural failure of soot-stained towers, the city is actually an amazing collection of traditional architecture, from the elaborate and symbolic buildings of temples and royal palaces to the residential teak homes that sheltered Thai families from the elements before the introduction of modern shophouses.

> BARS & CLUBS

Bangkok is a party animal – even on a tight leash. Back in 2001, the Thaksin administration started enforcing closing times and curtailing other excesses that made Bangkok famous. Since the 2006 ousting of Thaksin, the laws have been conveniently circumvented or inconsistently enforced, and several years on, the postcoup party scene has shown signs of restoring Bangkok to its old position as Southeast Asia's fun master, a role uptight Singapore almost usurped. But it is still common for the men in brown to switch on the lights in clubs and bars way before bedtime, or at least before dawn.

Officially bars and clubs close at 2am, but this is subject to police discretion. The drinking age is 20 years old and ID checks are even enforced on grey-haired patrons.

During the sanctioned hours, Bangkok's watering holes range from grubby suds joints to upscale cocktail dens. A quintessential Bangkok night includes filling a plastic outdoor table with emptied bottles of beer. Th Khao San (p61) and its connected streets remain the mama-san for partying backpackers and Thai hipsters. The yuppie crowd prefers to stay chic and air-conditioned in the internationally flavoured neighbourhoods of Sukhumvit and Silom.

The club scene is equally well versed in international trends, with lounge-style venues for vinyl spinners. Be warned though, the discos burn strong and bright on certain nights – a visit from a foreign DJ or the music flavour of the month – then hibernate on other nights. Clubs geared towards foreigners usually charge a cover of about 500B, while Thais will opt for clubs with a cheaper entrance fee. At the moment, the Thong Lor and Ekamai areas and RCA (Royal City Avenue) rule the nightscape for all ages and persuasions. Silom's gay discos still pack in the sweating bodies.

The curfew has done little to curb Bangkokians' night-owl tendencies. They don't hit the clubs until midnight, pursuing sà·nùk (fun) in a shortened time frame. Another consequence is the curiously creative methods of flouting closing times. Speakeasies have sprung up all over the city – follow the crowds, no one is heading home. Some places just remove the tables and let people drink on the floor (somehow this is an exemption), while other places serve beer in teapots. If it seems strange, welcome to Bangkok.

For more subdued tastes, Bangkok also attracts A-grade jazz musicians to several hotel bars. You'll find smokier riffs in elbow-tight rock-and-roll clubs scattered throughout the city.

Although Bangkok can party with global flair, let's not forget that prostitution landed it on the R&R map. During the 1980s, Patpong (Soi Patpong 1 and 2) earned notoriety for its wild sex shows, involving everything from ping-pong balls to razors to midgets on motorbikes. Today it is more of a circus for curious spectators than sexual deviants. Soi Cowboy and Nana Entertainment Plaza are the real scenes of sex for hire. Not all of the love-you-long-time business is geared towards Westerners: Soi Thaniya, off Th Silom, is filled with massage parlours for Japanese expats and visitors, while the immense massage parlours outside of central Bangkok attract Thai businessmen and officials.

AUSTIN BUSH / LONELY PLANET IMAGES ©

BEST BEER BARS & COCKTAIL LOUNGES
> Hippie de Bar (p63)
> Cheap Charlie's (p129)
> WTF (p130)
> Moon Bar at Vertigo (p112; pictured above)
> Coco Walk (p89)
> Soul Food Mahanakorn (p129)

BEST DANCE & MUSIC CLUBS
> Ad Here the 13th (p61)
> Tapas Room (p107)
> Brick Bar (p63)
> Ekamai Soi 5 (p131)
> Living Room (p131)
> 808 Club (p142)

SNAPSHOTS

> FOOD

It's a rare moment when Bangkok residents aren't eating, planning their next meal or swapping restaurant notes. Food is everywhere, from chic eateries to streetside stalls. The city's best restaurants are glorified family kitchens where dressing to impress means wiping down the laminate tables. And almost every corner of the city boasts a small army of street vendors ranging from speciality carts to the venerable name-that-dish maestros.

The classic Bangkok eating experience is sitting on a plastic stool by the side of a traffic-choked road and eating a bowl of noodles or a simple rice dish cooked in front of you. Locals, both rich and poor, will travel any distance to their favourite stall – it's not rare to see Mercedes parked alongside motorbikes at these stalls.

Once you opt for a Thai restaurant, you need to adopt a Thai frame of mind: ambience is overrated and courses are a foreign concept. Eating is a social occasion to be shared with as many people as possible. The head of the table typically orders a combination of dishes, which arrive in no particular order since they will be eaten family style. Foreigners who

Let the aromas guide you for breakfast, lunch, dinner and all that's in between

GREG ELMS / LONELY PLANET IMAGES ©

BEST UPMARKET RESTAURANTS
> nahm (p111)
> Sra Bua (p89)
> Le Normandie (p102)
> D'Sens (p111; pictured below)
> Bo.lan (p125)

BEST CASUAL RESTAURANTS
> Nay Mong (p76)
> Krua Apsorn (p58)
> MBK Food Court (p88)
> Soi 38 Night Market (p128)
> Kaloang Home Kitchen (p69)

AUSTIN BUSH / LONELY PLANET IMAGES ©

insist on ordering individually (and not sharing) are frequently frustrated by the kitchen's poor timing – a cross-cultural glitch, not incompetence.

While humble home-style restaurants are widespread throughout the city, finding an authentic Thai restaurant with enough ambience to qualify as a date is a tall order. Typically a beautiful setting is merely a disguise for an incompetent kitchen. When Thais celebrate a special occasion they opt for an import cuisine, such as Italian or Chinese-style seafood, instead of their everyday menu. The thinking goes something like this: why dress up meat and three veg when you could splurge on foie gras? Exotic cuisine is relative.

Of the foreign-born meals, Italian translates well into Bangkok's steamy climate and many Italian émigrés have successfully peddled their homeland's menus to noodle-loving Thais. Being a city of immigrants, Bangkok also boasts home-style restaurants from Arabia, India and China as well as various European nations to scratch an itch for home.

> SHOPPING & MARKETS

Even avowed anticonsumerists weaken in Bangkok. One minute they're touting the virtues of a life without material possessions, the next they're admiring the fake Rolex watches and mapping out the BTS route to Chatuchak Weekend Market. If you intend to launch a full-scale shopping assault, don't deny yourself a copy of Nancy Chandler's indispensable illustrated *Map of Bangkok,* widely available at local bookshops.

Let's first introduce you to Bangkok's mall culture. In some cities, frolicking outside is a common free-time activity, but in Bangkok's concrete landscape and humid climate the air-conditioned malls serve as city parks. Even if their credit cards don't measure up, every able-bodied Bangkokian is a de facto mall rat, strolling the halls of these consumer temples for people-watching and window-shopping.

There are of course class distinctions; this is a feudal society. The social-ites prefer the Emporium, the teens dig MBK, and everyone wanders into

PETER STUCKINGS / LONELY PLANET IMAGES ©

BEST FOR FASHION & DESIGN
> Siam Square (p87)
> Siam Center (p86)
> Nandakwang (p122)
> Central World Plaza (p82)
> Siam Discovery Center (p86)
> Propaganda (p123)

BEST FOR SOUVENIRS & GIFTS
> Chatuchak Weekend Market (p138; pictured above)
> Thai Home Industries (p101)
> Gaysorn Plaza (p83)
> Khao San Market (p55)
> Narai Phand (p84)

Colour coordinate your kitchenware at Propaganda (p123)

RICHARD I'ANSON / LONELY PLANET IMAGES ©

Siam Paragon for a photo-op in front of the ground-floor fountain. Most malls are anchored by a department store (Tokyu, Zen, Sogo etc) that gets pawed by bargain hunters during periodic sales, but the busiest part is the food court because Thais live to eat.

You'll find mainly international chains in the malls, but Bangkok has a growing collection of local designer brands that combine city chic with Thai fabrics and aesthetics to produce clubwear, daywear and artwear.

The malls, however, are just a warm-up for the markets, the cardio workout of shopping. In Bangkok, footpaths are for additional retail space not for pedestrians, and where there are walkers, there are vendors. Streetside markets dominate in tourist areas, such as Th Sukhumvit, Th Silom and Th Khao San, selling everything a luggage carrier would want. Don't forget to stroll the everyday markets to see the wants and needs of Thai households.

What else can you buy in the City of Heavenly Bargains? Thanks to the diplomatic corps, Bangkok also has a sartorial tradition. As one of the world's biggest exporters of gems and ornaments, Thailand offers some good buys if you know what you're doing. Both suits and gems are prone to prolific scams so shop responsibly.

> TEMPLES & SHRINES

Although famous for its hedonism, Bangkok is more devout than debauched. Thai Buddhism's most important figure – the king, himself – resides here, as do the central temples and Buddha figures associated with the god incarnate. Below this sacred plane is the daily practice of religion, comprising local temples, famous shrines and household altars.

The older districts of Ko Ratanakosin, Thonburi and Banglamphu are the primary sightseeing spots for temple tours. Here the spires of the mosaic-covered stupas are often the tallest towers in sight. There are of course the famous temples – Wat Phra Kaew, Wat Arun and Wat Pho – but to get a true sense of a temple's role in the community, visit the

Monks in morning prayer at Wat Pho (p44)

RICHARD I'ANSON / LONELY PLANET IMAGES ©

BEST TEMPLES & SHRINES
> Wat Pho (p44)
> Wat Phra Kaew (p42; pictured below)
> Wat Arun (p44)
> Wat Mangkon Kamalawat (p73)
> Erawan Shrine (p80)
> Wat Saket & Golden Mount (p54)

BEST SPOTS TO STUDY MEDITATION
> World Fellowship of Buddhists (p120)
> Wat Mahathat's International Buddhist Meditation Centre (p46)
> House of Dhamma (p137)

RICHARD I'ANSON / LONELY PLANET IMAGES ©

noncelebrities. Here you'll find clotheslines covered in freshly laundered monks' robes, dusty yards populated by a lazy stray dog and a brood of chickens, and Thai matrons in their finest silks making merit. In the early morning, novice monks traverse the neighbourhoods in bare feet collecting alms for their day's meal.

Religious devotion is not confined to the whitewashed temple walls. In Bangkok, sacred spaces are as prolific as traffic jams. Thailand's version of Buddhism is heavily spiced with animistic spirit worship. These spirits dwell in earthly spaces and are often given their own residences, in the case of the spirit houses and shrines occupying homes or businesses. Spirits that tinker with fate and fortune are often appeased with daily offerings of food and drink set out upon a doorstep or a dedicated altar within the home.

Even the body is transformed into a walking altar – most Thais wear amulets to protect them from harm and ensure good fortune. For taxi and bus drivers, their vehicles become moving temples displaying stickers of famous monks and flower-garland offerings. Treating the unknown forces of fate with respect might appear to be more important than obeying traffic rules.

Chinatown provides an interesting counterpoint to Thai Buddhism. Ancestor worship plays a larger role in Chinese Buddhism and morning rituals often include the burning of paper offerings, in streetside bins, to the deceased.

> GAY & LESBIAN BANGKOK

In anything-goes Bangkok, gays and lesbians enjoy an unprecedented amount of acceptance considering the conservative views of the region. Gay professionals enjoy relative equality in the workplace and a pride parade is celebrated annually with great fanfare. Homosexual couples, as well as straight couples, do not show public affection, unless they are purposefully flouting social mores.

A long-standing social phenomenon in Thailand is the third gender (*gà·teui*), often translated into English as 'ladyboy'. Some are cross-dressers, while others have had sexual-reassignment surgery. (Thailand is one of the leading countries for this procedure.) Regardless of their anatomy, most *gà·teui* assume an exaggerated feminine persona, often wearing more make-up than Thai women. Foreigners are especially fascinated by ladyboys as they are often very convincing women, and *gà·teui* cabarets aimed at tourists are popular venues for observing gender bending.

In terms of nightlife, Bangkok has a well-defined pink triangle around Th Silom. Dead-end Soi 2 is packed with pretty-boy discos, while Soi 4 has the people-watching bars. There is a local Thai scene along Th Kamphaeng Phet, near Chatuchak.

Bangkok used to ignore lesbians (known locally as *tom-dee*), but that has changed with the emergence of Zeta, a female-only club in the RCA (Royal City Avenue) area.

For more leads on Bangkok's gay scene, check out Utopia (www.utopia-asia.com), which lists Bangkok events and goings-on.

AUSTIN BUSH / LONELY PLANET IMAGES ©

BEST...
> For people-watching: Balcony Bar (p105) and Telephone (p106)
> For sweating to techno: DJ Station (p106)
> For shirtless dancing: G.O.D. (p106; pictured right)
> For the girls: Zeta (p142)

> SPAS & WELLNESS CENTRES

This city aims to please. Add in a tradition of massage and a favourable currency exchange rate and you've got yourself a spa date. Spa treatments that might cost a small fortune in any other metropolis are thankfully discounted in the City of Angelic Prices. Bangkok's day spas are also up to speed on all of the international techniques: you can be kneaded like dough, bathed in mud, dunked in flowers and wrapped in seaweed. Tony Chi's minimalist spa designs enjoy a Bangkok address, as do traditional Thai-style homes transformed into gardens of tranquillity. You can visit a full-on spa cottage, with in-room treatments, or just enjoy a couple's package overlooking the Bangkok skyline. More down-market are the little storefronts that will pluck and wax errant hairs, sculpt talons into nails and tint away hints of grey. Beauty runs a close second behind food as a citywide obsession.

If you need more than an image upgrade, Bangkok can oblige. Medical tourism, an apparent oxymoron, is a booming business here. Bangkok's hospitals are on par with top-tier Western facilities and cover all the bases – including dentistry, nips and tucks, corrective and elective surgeries – for less than the price at home. Some folks mix medical with pleasure by scheduling a procedure they couldn't afford at home with a recuperative stay at a nearby beach resort.

More recently, wellness centres have begun to offer a combination of Western and alternative therapies to address weight problems and substance addiction.

BEST...
> For jet-lag massage: Oriental Spa Thai Health & Beauty Centre (p96)
> For honeymoon couples: Banyan Tree Spa (p110)
> For spa cottages: Coran Boutique Spa (p119)
> For Thai elegance: Divana Massage & Spa (p119)
> For health treatments: Rasayana Retreat (p120)
> For no-nonsense haircuts: Take Care (p120)
> For an intimate day spa: Spa 1930 (p81)

> TRADITIONAL MASSAGE

Once you've been stretched, pulled, kneaded and pinched, you'll realise why a Thai massage isn't the luxurious indulgence you might expect. Thailand's interpretation is a combination of yoga and acupressure resulting in a passive workout. Although a foot in your armpit might not be your idea of relaxation, these leverlike positions are time-tested for unclogging energy meridians and promoting health. Devotees describe a comfortable euphoria setting in after a particularly forceful session and some even use massage to treat chronic pain and disease. In fact, massage is considered a vital component to overall health, as necessary as diet and exercise.

There is no shortage of massage shops in Bangkok, but not all are created equally. Some blur the line between ancient massage and 'recreation' (often providing happy endings for male patrons), while others are massage assembly lines with a constant stream of prostrate bodies. For men who wish to avoid a massage surprise, look for a parlour employing old ladies rather than pretty young things.

There is also a huge menu of massage styles; eg foot, full body and full body with oil or herbal compresses. Although the masseuses might seem demure, their fingers are like steel vices that can manipulate brawny patrons into puddles of jelly. Any massage is good, but finding a great massage depends on matching your personal threshold for pain with the masseuse's grip. No pain, no gain is the mantra of some, while others prefer to be pummelled more tenderly. Most, however, will agree that a massage a day will keep the doctor (or at least the aches) away.

BEST...

> For Thai-style herbal compress massages: Asia Herb Association (p119)
> For studying Thai massage: Wat Pho Thai Traditional Medical & Massage School (p46)
> For post-shopping massage: Thann Sanctuary (p81)
> For treating generic aches: Healthland Spa & Massage (p96)
> For a traditional Thai setting: Ruen-Nuad Massage Studio (p97)

 >BACKGROUND

GREG ELMS / LONELY PLANET IMAGES ©
A river cruise reveals some awe-inspiring sights, such as Wat Pho (p44)

HISTORY
A SIAMESE CAPITAL

Bangkok is the phoenix-risen of the Thai kingdom, the second chance after the nation's thriving capital, Ayuthaya, was devastated by Burmese invaders in 1767. In the ensuing collapse, General Taksin emerged as the primary leader, forcing out the Burmese and establishing a new capital in Thonburi, on the western bank of Mae Nam Chao Phraya. Taksin's reunification of the country was decisive, but his ruling style was ruthless. By 1782, Chao Phraya Chakri, a key general, deposed Taksin as king and moved the capital across the river to modern-day Bangkok. Chakri's son inherited the throne, thus establishing the Chakri dynasty, which is still in place today.

Chao Phraya Chakri (also known as Rama I and King Buddha Yodfa) chose the eastern bank of the river as a defensive measure against possible Burmese invasions. *Khlong* (canals) were dug to replicate the island-city of Ayuthaya and artisans were commissioned to build great temples to replace those destroyed in the old capital. The waterways were a key element in the cycle of life.

Reforms during the mid-19th and early 20th centuries – enacted by Rama IV (King Mongkut; r 1851–68) and his son, Rama V (King Chulalongkorn; r 1868–1910) – took the country into the modern era. Changes included the creation of a civil service, still one of Bangkok's biggest employers, eradication of slavery and successful defence of Thailand's independence during European colonisation.

You'd never know it today, but Bangkok's first road (Th Charoen Krung, also known as the 'New Road') wasn't built until the 1860s. As motorised transport took off, Bangkok expanded in every direction, often building over former canals.

The political landscape changed rapidly, too, with a bloodless coup in 1932 abruptly ending the era of absolute monarchy and ushering in a constitutional monarchy. Then in 1939 the country's official name changed from Siam to Thailand. Bangkok's infamous sex industry expanded during the Vietnam War, when it was a popular R&R stop for foreign troops.

In the 1970s, democracy was on a shaky path – the military brutally suppressed a prodemocracy student rally in Bangkok and the country later see-sawed between civilian and military rule. In May 1992, large demonstrations calling for the resignation of Thai army leader General

Suchinda Kraprayoon saw violent street confrontations near Democracy Monument, resulting in 50 civilian deaths. After a right royal scolding from the king, Kraprayoon resigned. For the rest of the decade, parliament was dominated by the Democrat Party.

BANGKOK TODAY

In the last decades of the 20th century, Bangkok was the beating heart of one of Asia's hottest economies. Modern skyscrapers tickled the skyline, and the middle and upper classes flaunted Western luxury goods. But in 1997 the bubble burst and the Thai currency spiralled ever downwards. By the new millennium, the Thai economy was back on track, showing more sustainable growth than in the boom-and-bust years.

The city continued to mature by developing two public transit systems: the BTS (Skytrain) and MRT (Metro) subway, both of which were civic-minded novelties to the traffic-choked city. Campaigns to 'clean up the city' – be it crackdowns on police corruption or early closing times for bars – were spearheaded by former prime minister Thaksin Shinawatra.

The 1997 passage of a national constitution ensured increased human and civil rights and was supposed to signal Thailand's successful coming-of-age as a democracy. It was abolished in 2006 during the country's most recent coup to unseat then prime minister Thaksin Shinawatra, a telecommunications billionaire, and his Thai Rak Thai (Thais Love Thais) party. Thaksin had swept into power in 2001 on a populist platform widely supported by rural voters.

By 2005 his party had won a larger majority of the National Assembly, effectively creating one-party rule in the kingdom. Bangkok's intellectuals alleged that Thaksin used his power to suppress media

---

TONGUE-TWISTING TITLE

At 26 words long, Bangkok's Thai name is a bit of a mouthful, so everyone shortens it to 'Krung Thep', or 'City of Angels'. The full-length version can be translated as: 'Great city of angels, the repository of divine gems, the great land unconquerable, the grand and prominent realm, the royal and delightful capital full of nine noble gems, the highest royal dwelling and grand palace, the divine shelter and living place of reincarnated spirits'. Foreigners, however, never bothered to learn either and continued to call the capital 'Bang Makok' (Village of Olive Plums), which was eventually truncated to 'Bangkok'.

freedoms and pass legislation that favoured his and his cronies' commercial ventures.

Political theatre dominated 2006 and 2007. Bangkok street protesters rang in the new year of 2006 calling for Thaksin's resignation over the tax-free sale of his family's telecommunications business (Shin Corporation), as well as suspicions that he had ambitions to assume the throne from the current and ageing king. Thaksin challenged his critics by dissolving parliament and calling for new elections that would prove his popular mandate.

Before legitimate elections were held, military tanks rolled into Bangkok and told Thaksin, who was in New York at the time, not to come back. The city initially rejoiced after its 'liberation', and coup leaders promised speedy elections with a new and improved constitution.

Military rule persisted for more than a year, and elections in late 2007 led to the party of an alleged Thaksin proxy, Samak Sundaravej, assuming power. Samak would eventually be the first of four prime ministers during 2007–08, a period defined largely by political instability, and culminating, in late 2008, in the taking over of Bangkok's international airport by a group of yellow-shirted anti-Thaksin protesters.

After a great deal of political wrangling, a tenuous coalition was formed in December 2008, led by Oxford-educated Abhisit Vejjajiva, leader of the Democrat Party. Despite being young, photogenic and allegedly untainted by corruption, Abhisit's perceived association with the yellow shirts did little to placate the pro-Thaksin camp.

In February 2010, after Thaksin's remaining Thai assets were seized by the Supreme Court, yet another round of protests began. Thaksin supporters and self-proclaimed prodemocracy advocates, all sporting red shirts, united in Bangkok to demand that Prime Minister Abhisit Vejjajiva stand down.

The protests remained largely peaceful until April, when there were violent clashes between police and protesters (numbering up to tens of thousands), which resulted in 25 deaths. Protesters barricaded themselves into an area stretching from Lumphini Park to the shopping district near Siam Square, effectively shutting down parts of central Bangkok. In May the protesters were dispersed by force, but not before at least 36 buildings (including Central World Plaza) were set alight and at least 15 people killed. The death toll from the 2010 conflicts amounted to 91 people, making it Thailand's most violent political unrest in 20 years.

In July 2011, the red-/yellow-shirt conflict came to the forefront again, in the form of parliamentary elections. Due to Thaksin's enduring popularity, the red shirt–linked Pheu Thai party dominated, winning 265 of 500 seats. Its candidate for prime minister, Yingluck Shinawatra, Thaksin's younger sister and a political novice, raises the possibility of a return of her exiled brother to Thailand, and further political instability in the country.

LIFE AS A BANGKOK RESIDENT
CITY OF ANGELS

Bangkok is both utterly Thai and totally foreign. Old and new ways clash and mingle, constantly redrawing the lines of what it means to be 'Thai'. The city has a huge concentration of citizens with disposable income, from the empire princesses of the hi-so (high society) scene to the teen-agers hanging out in Siam Square. In certain circles, Bangkok will seem decidedly Westernised, with bilingual, foreign-educated Thais more familiar with *The Simpsons* than squat toilets. But despite the international veneer, a Thai value system – built primarily on religious and monarchical devotion – is ticking away, guiding every aspect of life. Almost all Thais, even the most conspicuously consuming, are dedicated Buddhists who aim to be reborn into a better life by making merit (giving donations to temples or feeding monks), regarding merit-making as the key to their earthly success.

Bangkok accommodates every rung of the economic ladder, from the aristocrat to the slum dweller. It is the new start for the economic hopefuls and the last chance for the economic refugees. The lucky ones from the bottom rung form the working class backbone of the city – taxi drivers, food vendors, maids, nannies and even prostitutes. Many hail from the northeastern provinces and send hard-earned baht

---

DID YOU KNOW?
> Women constitute half of the workforce in Bangkok.
> Bangkok's minimum daily wage is 206B (US$6.76).
> Bangkok was rated the world's hottest city (in terms of temperature) by the World Meteorological Organization.
> Rama IX (King Bhumibol; r 1946–) is the world's longest-reigning monarch.

back to their families in small rural villages. At the very bottom are the dispossessed, who live in squatter communities on marginal, often polluted land. While the Thai economy has surged, a social net has yet to be constructed. Meanwhile, Bangkok is also the great incubator for Thailand's new generation of young creatives, from designers to architects, and has long nurtured the archetype of the country's middle class.

The city has also represented economic opportunity for foreign immigrants. Approximately a quarter of the city's population claims some Chinese ancestry, be it Cantonese, Hainanese, Hokkien or Teochew. Although the first Chinese labourers faced discrimination from the Thais, their descendants' success in business, finance and public affairs helped to elevate the status of Chinese and Thai-Chinese families. In fact, many of the ruling mercantile families are Thai-Chinese and even the present king has some Chinese heritage.

Immigrants from South Asia also migrated to Bangkok and comprise the second-largest Asian minority. Sikhs from northern India typically make their living in tailoring, while Sinhalese, Bangladeshis, Nepalis and Pakistanis can be found in the import-export or retail trades.

MONARCHY

The Thais' relationship with their king is deeply spiritual and intensely personal. Many view him as a god (all Thai kings are referred to as 'Rama', one of the incarnations of the Hindu god Vishnu) and as a father figure (the king's birthday is the national celebration of Father's Day). The reigning monarch, King Bhumibol Adulyadej, inherited automatic reverence when he assumed the throne, but he captured the Thai people's hearts with his actions. When he was younger, he was fashionable and photogenic: scooting around town in a yellow Rolls-Royce (yellow is the colour associated with the day of the week the king was born) and playing jazz saxophone. He embodied the ideal modern Thai, cultured and cosmopolitan yet respectful of tradition. His role as a figurehead of the nation was augmented with his role as a provider and protector through well-publicised projects aimed at the country's struggling farmers.

Pictures of the king and the queen line the royal avenue of Th Ratchadamnoen and many Thais will *wâi* (traditional Thai greeting) the pictures as they pass on their daily commute. Drivers also decorate their cars with bumper stickers that read: 'We Love the King'.

In June 2006, the king celebrated his 60th year on the throne, an event regarded by many Thais as bittersweet because the ageing king (now 83 years old) may soon leave the helm of the Thai nation. His son, Crown Prince Maha Vajiralongkorn, has been chosen to succeed him, but it is the king's daughter, Princess Mahachakri Sirindhorn, that many Thais feel a deeper connection with because she has followed in her father's philanthropic footsteps.

ETIQUETTE

Just remember to respect two things: religion and the monarchy. This means standing when the national or royal anthem is played (before movies and at 8am and 6pm daily); not criticising the king or his family; and dressing respectfully at royal buildings and temples (with shoulders and legs covered, and shoes removed before entering buildings). Keep your feet pointed away from a Buddha image. Monks aren't supposed to touch or be touched by women.

Other ways to avoid offending Thais include not wearing shoes inside people's homes; not touching anyone's head; and keeping your feet and shoes on the floor, not on a chair or table. Remember to keep your cool, as getting angry or talking loudly is thought rude. Losing your temper is considered a major loss of face for both parties. The better approach is to speak softly and smile – Thais are suckers for a good smile.

Pedestrian behaviour in Bangkok can be off-putting for Westerners accustomed to more orderly street etiquette. Remember that pedestrians have no rights when interacting with cars, motorcycles or even push-carts. When crossing a street stalled with traffic, look between the lanes for speeding motorcycles.

WHEN TO WÂI

Elegant and complicated, the traditional Thai greeting is the *wâi,* a gesture where palms are put together, prayerlike. The placement of the hands in relation to the face is a delicate formula, dependent on the status of the two people *wâi*-ing each other. Thais don't expect foreigners to understand these rules, but it is polite to return a *wâi* to a friend, coworker and definitely to a VIP. The biggest mistake made by foreigners is to throw out a *wâi* to every door attendant. When you are the customer, you don't *wâi* the server – that means the noodle vendor, tailor and concierge, even if you're really happy.

ART & ARCHITECTURE

Both a modern metropolis and a traditional village, Bangkok provides a glimpse into the artistic treasures of the Thai kingdom.

TEMPLES & TOWERS

Sitting in the river delta of the central plains, Bangkok was built beside the river or canals by a people who knew how to cope with the monsoon rains and seasonal flooding. Traditional teak homes were built on stilts, either single-room houses or interconnected by walkways. Rooflines were steep and often decorated with spiritual motifs. The functional elements of traditional construction protected the homes from waterways that jumped their banks during the rainy season. And when the water dried up and the sun beat down, the undercarriage of the homes provided a shady and breezy escape.

In the realm of cultural artisanship, Thailand's energies were channelled into temple (wat) architecture. Of the core components of a temple complex, the *chedi* (stupa, where holy relics are stored) is a poignant example of outside influences in early Thai history. A bell-shaped *chedi* is often credited to the style of Ceylon (Sri Lanka), which participated with Thailand in many monastic exchanges, and the corn-cob-shaped *prang* (tower) is an inheritance from the Khmer empire. The dazzling colours and sparkling mosaics are all Thai.

Around the 19th century, Bangkok adopted the Sino Portuguese–style shophouses and warehouses that lined the waterways of neighbouring port cities such as Singapore and Penang. Traditional elements were mixed with these neoclassical trends and dubbed Ratanakosin (or old Bangkok) style. The old ministry buildings in Ko Ratanakosin are leading examples. Later, Thai techniques merged with Victorian sentiments in the feminine confection of buildings at Dusit Palace Park (p67).

The city started growing skyward in the 1970s. First slowly with the Dusit Thani Hotel on Th Silom, which climbed higher than the city's temple spires, and then in a mad rush during the close of the millennium. By the year 2000, nearly a thousand buildings could claim the same distinction, with at least 20 of them towering higher than 45 floors. The most flamboyant of the late 1980s is the former headquarters of the Bank of Asia, better known as the Robot Building, on Th Sathon Tai. The building's facade is decorated with industrial components, suggesting a supersized robot. If you get enough altitude on the city, you'll also spot a building with the silhouette of an elephant. The towers that followed this playful period are more subdued geometric structures. The tallest scraper in the Bangkok (and the country's) skyline is the Baiyoke Tower, which is unfortunately dwarfed in the region by Kuala Lumpur's Petronas Twin Towers.

VISUAL ARTS

Thailand's most famous contribution to the world of art has been Buddha sculptures. Traditional Thai painting was limited to intricate representations of the *Ramakian* (Thailand's version of India's epic *Ramayana*) and *Jataka* (tales of the Buddha's past lives), painted as sermons on temple walls.

Italian artist Corrado Feroci is often credited for jump-starting Thailand's secular art movement. He designed the Democracy Monument and developed the first fine-arts department, now at Silpakorn University. Bangkok continues to foster Thailand's avant-garde. Internationally known Montien Boonma uses abstract symbolism to revisit traditional Buddhist themes. Reactionary artists, such as Manit Sriwanichpoom, often mix pop aesthetics with social commentary. Thaweesak Srithongdee's cheeky superheroes and sculptor Manop Suwanpinta's human anatomy pieces are confoundingly meaningless yet profound.

THEATRE & DANCE

The stage in Thailand typically hosts a *khon* performance, one of the six traditional dramatic forms. It's extravagant and a visual feast, where hundreds of masked characters love and die, fight and dance. Acted only by men, *khon* drama is based upon stories of the *Ramakian* and was traditionally only for royal audiences.

The less formal *lá·kon* dances, of which there are many dying sub-genres, usually involve costumed dancers (of both sexes) performing elements of the *Ramakian* and traditional folk tales. The most widespread variation is called *lá·kon gâa bon,* which is commissioned by worshippers at shrines to earn merit.

Royal marionettes *(lá·kon lék),* once on the brink of extinction, have been revived by Aksra Theatre (p141). The metre-high creations are elaborately costumed and perform all the subtle manipulations required of their human *khon* counterparts.

MUSIC

The traditional Thai orchestra *(bèe·pâht)* is made up of the rhythmic clinking of cymbals, the whine of the stringed *saw* and the playful rain sounds

---

BKK HIT-LIST

Need to know who's who in Bangkok's musical soundscape? Poets, punks and pop stars get top billing.

> *That Song* (Modern Dog) – Thailand's grunge gurus' album features the hit song 'Dta Sawang' (Clear Eyes).
> *Made in Thailand* (Carabao) – the classic Thai rock album. Check out the eponymous song's English chorus.
> *Kon Gap Kwai* (Caravan) – considered one of the first albums of *pleng pêua chee·wít* (songs for life).
> *Best* (Pumpuang Duanjan) – a collection of songs from *lôok tûng's* (literally 'children of the fields') diva.
> *I Believe* (Tata Young) – Thailand's pop goddess won international fans with this English-language album, full of snappy tweener hits.
> *Best of Loso* (Loso) – an introduction to the songs that most Thais can sing by heart.

---

of the *rá·nâht èhk* (wooden xylophone), along with another five to 20 instruments. The snake-charmer sounds of the *bèe* (oboe-like woodwind) usually accompanies Thai-boxing matches.

Modern Thai music ranges from sappy pop tunes and heartbreaking ballads to protest songs. Taxi drivers love the *lôok tûng* (literally 'children of the fields') music genre, from the rural northeastern provinces. There's a definite croon feel to it, though the subject matter mines the faithful country-and-western themes of losing your job, your wife and your buffalo. Rock bands Carabao and Caravan have earned legendary status for their politically charged songs, termed *pleng pêua chee·wít* (songs for life).

Today the alternative hordes are celebrating the amorphic genre of indie, including everything from alt-rock, rap and ska-funk recorded on independent labels. Tune into the radio station 104.5FM Fat Radio or catch weekend shows at Centrepoint Plaza (Siam Square Soi 7 between Soi 3 and Soi 4) or Th Khao San for the latest Thai indie music.

GOVERNMENT & POLITICS

Bangkok is the seat of the national government, based on the British system of constitutional monarchy. In 2007 voters approved a military-drafted constitution – the country's 17th since abolishing absolute monarchy in 1932. Since then, Thailand has seen four prime ministers, one appointed by royal command, and is set for a fifth. The prime minister designate, Yingluck Shinawatra of the Pheu Thai party, came to power via a parliamentary vote and is expected to take office in mid-2011.

The city is administered by a popularly elected governor and is divided into 50 districts (called *kèht*) and 154 subdistricts (called *kwăang*). Bangkok is typically more liberal than the rest of the country, but clear political distinctions exist between the working class and the elite. The 2004 win of the Bangkok gubernatorial election by Democrat Apirak Kosayodhin was widely regarded as a protest vote by the citizens of the capital against the authoritarian style of then prime minister Thaksin Shinawatra and his populist Thai Rak Thai party.

In the 2006 district elections, Democrats won additional support, garnering 61% of the seats. Governor Apirak's city administration was eventually implicated in several corruption scandals regarding city contracts, and in 2008 Apirak Kosayodhin resigned. Subsequent elections led to fellow Democrat, MR Sukhumbhand Paribatra, at press time still Bangkok's governor, taking office.

ENVIRONMENT

We won't lie to you – Bangkok is polluted. The combination of tropical heat and air pollution will leave you covered in sweat and gasping for fresh air. The air quality becomes most stultifying at major intersections, with asphyxiating vehicle emissions and particulate matter. Over the past 10 years, Bangkok has eradicated much of the most toxic elements of air pollution – lead and sulphur dioxide – but still struggles with dangerous levels of particulate matter created by automobiles and construction projects.

Bangkok is also a damned noisy place round the clock, as you'll discover if you stay near a construction site jumping with jackhammers. Screaming motorcycles and thundering buses also comprise the Bangkok symphony that often blots out streetside conversations.

There has been an effort to clean up the waterways over recent decades. The results are most noticeable in the river, still used daily by residents for bathing, laundry and drinking water (after treatment). The canals on the Bangkok side are particularly murky and are still used as garbage disposals. When riding the *khlong* taxi, locals cover their faces with handkerchiefs or crouch behind the adjustable plastic tarp when the boat hits an errant wave.

FURTHER READING & FILMS

Much of the literature that shapes Bangkok's modern psyche has not been translated into English. One of the few exceptions set in Bangkok is *Married to the Demon King,* translated and notated by Susan Fulop Kepner and based on Sri Daoruang's tale of a modern-day Bangkok marriage drawing from the epic characters of the *Ramakian.*

Most Thais are avid comic-book readers but rarely commit themselves to publications with more meat. The city's bookshops are also well stocked with art and design magazines, catering to the recent obsession with style and commercial design.

In addition to the many books that decipher Thai culture for Western readers, *Very Thai: Everyday Pop Culture,* by Philip Cornwel-Smith, explains in a series of essays Bangkok's many oddities from taxi shrines to the city's obsession with uniforms. *Bangkok,* by William Warren, isn't so much a cultural exploration as an historical memoir and tribute to the city. *Vanishing Bangkok,* a photo-essay by Surat Osathanugrah, documents the activities in and around the city's disappearing canals.

In the novel department, most English-language books about Bangkok are dominated by formulaic sex-capades, dealing mainly with brothels and gangsters. The most insightful is the hard-boiled crime thriller *Bangkok 8,* by John Burdett, whose hero is a collection of opposites: a Thai *fa·ràng* cop who grew up in the brothels but matured in the monastery. *Jasmine Nights,* by SP Somtow, follows the coming-of-age of an upper-middle-class Bangkok teenager. *Sightseeing,* by Rattawut Lapcharoensap, is a collection of short stories about functional and dysfunctional families in Bangkok.

When it comes to Thai cinema, there are some exceptional stories that poignantly capture Bangkok and then there's lots of mediocre fluff that requires a deep appreciation of Thailand rather than good cinema. You are usually in good hands with any films made by Pen-Ek Ratanaruang, one of the country's leading alt-film directors. His debut film was *Fun Bar Karaoke,* a 1997 satire of Bangkok life in which the main characters are an ageing Thai playboy and his daughter. *Mon Rak Transistor* (2001) spins the tragicomic odyssey of a young villager who tries to crack the big time *lôok tûng* music scene in Bangkok. But it will be the atmospheric tale of *Ruang Rak Noi Nid Mahasan* (*Last Life in the Universe;* 2003), written by Prabda Yoon, that will secure Pen-Ek's work a position in cinema classics.

>DIRECTORY
TRANSPORT
ARRIVAL & DEPARTURE

Bangkok is a major regional travel hub. No-frills, low-cost airlines have also sprouted for short hops within Thailand and the region. Bus and train services are comfortable and affordable, albeit slower.

AIR

All international flights operate from Suvarnabhumi (Bangkok International) Airport, but the old Don Muang Airport continues to handle certain domestic flights. To avoid confusion, be sure to check with the ticketing agent or airline about which airport your domestic flights will be using.

Suvarnabhumi (Bangkok International) Airport

Located 25km east of the city, Suvarnabhumi (pronounced *sù·wan·ná·poom*) airport opened in 2006. For general inquiries, contact ☎ 0 2132 1888 or www. bangkokairportonline.com.

The airport is accessible by both highway links and a new airport train link, and estimated transit time to central Bangkok is 30 to 45 minutes.

Metered taxis are available curbside at the 1st floor – ignore the 'official airport taxi' touts who approach you inside the terminal. Typical metered fares from the airport are as follows: 200B to 250B to Th Sukhumvit; 250B to 300B to Th Khao San; 500B to Mo Chit. Toll charges (paid by the passengers) vary between 25B and 45B. Note that there's an additional 50B surcharge added to all fares departing from the airport, payable to the driver.

You can hail a taxi directly from the street for airport trips or you can arrange one through the hotels or by calling ☎ 1681 (which charges a 20B dispatch surcharge).

In 2010 the elevated train service linking central Bangkok and Suvarnabhumi Airport was finally completed. The system is comprised of a local service, which makes six stops before terminating at Phaya Thai station (30 minutes, 45B), connected by a walkway to the BTS at Phaya Thai station, and an express service that runs between Makkasan station and Suvarnabhumi Airport (15 minutes, 150B).

Makkasan, also known as Bangkok City Air Terminal, is a short walk from Phetchaburi MRT station, and if you show up at least three hours before your departure, also has check-in facilities for three different airlines (Thai Airways, Bangkok Airways and Lufthansa).

CLIMATE CHANGE & TRAVEL

Every form of transport that relies on carbon-based fuel generates CO_2, the main cause of human-induced climate change. Modern travel is dependent on aeroplanes, which might use less fuel per kilometre per person than most cars but travel much greater distances. The altitude at which aircraft emit gases (including CO_2) and particles also contributes to their climate change impact. Many websites offer 'carbon calculators' that allow people to estimate the carbon emissions generated by their journey and, for those who wish to do so, to offset the impact of the greenhouse gases emitted with contributions to portfolios of climate-friendly initiatives throughout the world. Lonely Planet offsets the carbon footprint of all staff and author travel.

Both lines run from 6am to midnight.

Airport express buses operate along three routes between the airport and central Bangkok between 6.10am and 9pm. The cost is 150B. Route AE1 travels to Hualamphong, AE2 to Th Khao San and AE3 to Th Sukhumvit.

A public transport centre is 3km from the airport and includes a bus terminal with buses to a handful of provinces and inner-city-bound buses and minivans. Bus lines that city-bound travellers are likely to use include 551 (Victory Monument), 554 (Don Muang) and 556 (Th Khao San), and minivan line 552 (On Nut BTS station, 25B). From these points, you can continue on public transport or taxi to your hotel.

An airport shuttle running both an ordinary and express route connects the transport centre with the passenger terminals.

Don Muang Airport (formerly Bangkok International Airport)

Don Muang Airport, 20km north of Bangkok, services the following domestic carriers: Nok Air, Solar Air and One-Two-Go.

For general inquiries and flight information, contact ☎ 0 2535 1111 or www.donmuangairport online.com.

The airport is across the highway from Don Muang train station (accessible via an elevated walkway from the terminal). Trains travel to Bangkok's Hualamphong station roughly every hour or 1½ hours from 4am to 11.30am and then again every hour from 2pm to 9.30pm (3rd class ordinary/express 5/10B, one hour).

A metered taxi trip from the airport into the middle of Bangkok should cost you around 200B to 300B, plus tolls (20B to 45B) and a 50B airport fee. Don't be shy in telling the driver to put the meter on.

As of writing, the only transport options between an international flight at Suvarnabhumi and a domestic flight at Don Muang are taxi, minivan (50B, 6am to 9pm) or bus 554 from Suvarnabhumi's public transport centre. Considering the vagaries of traffic, we would not recommend trying to make an international–domestic transfer in one day if your flight is departing from Don Muang or vice versa.

BUS

Government and private buses do trips from Bangkok to cities around Thailand, as well as to Malaysia. For long-distance trips, buses departing from the government-bus terminals are more reliable and safer than buses leaving from tourist centres (such as Th Khao San).

Northern & Northeastern bus terminal (Map p134, D1; ☎ for northern routes 0 2936 2841, ext 311 & 442, for northeastern routes 0 2936 2841, ext 611 & 448; Th Kamphaeng Phet) is just northwest of Chatuchak Park. It's also commonly called Mo Chit station. Buses depart from here for northern and northeastern destinations such as Chiang Mai and Ayuthaya. To reach the bus terminal, take BTS to Mo Chit or the MRT to Chatuchak Park and transfer onto city bus 3, 77 or 509.

Eastern bus terminal (Map p116, H6; ☎ 0 2391 2504; Soi 40/Soi Ekamai, Th Sukhumvit) is the departure point for buses to Pattaya and Ban Phe, the boat pier to Ko Samet. Most people call it Ekamai station. The BTS stops at its own Ekkamai station in front of Soi 40.

Southern bus terminal (off Map p134; ☎ 0 2435 1199; cnr Th Bromaratchacho-nanee & Th Phuttamonthon 1, Thonburi), located 12km west of the Chao Phraya River, handles buses south to Phuket, Surat Thani and closer centres to the west such as Damnoen Saduak. This station is known as Sai Tai Mai. The easiest way to get here is by taxi, or you can take bus 79, 159, 201 or 516 from Th Ratchadamnoen or bus 40 from the Victory Monument.

TRAIN

From Hualamphong station, the main train station in Bangkok, there are five rail spurs – north to Chiang Mai, northeast to Nong Khai and Ubon Ratchathani (two lines that split at Khorat), south-east to Aranya Prathet (a border crossing point to Cambodia) and south to Malaysia.

Hualamphong has left-luggage facilities, although it is probably wiser to arrange this service at your hotel. In Thonburi, Bangkok Noi train station handles short-line routes to Kanchanaburi; there are no left-luggage facilities here.

To reserve seats or get time-table information, call the free 24-hour hotline ☎ 1690, visit www.railway.co.th or go directly to the advance-booking office at Hualamphong. Trains come in three classes – from cattle car to comfy fold-out beds. The website www.seat61.com has helpful train-planning advice.

TRAVEL DOCUMENTS

To enter Thailand, your passport must be valid for six months from the date of entry.

VISA

Residents of Australia, Canada, New Zealand, South Africa, the UK and the USA can stay in Thailand for 30 days without a visa if arriving by air. If you plan on a longer trip, apply for a 60-day tourist visa or a 90-day nonimmigrant visa before you leave home.

You can also apply for a visa extension from the **Immigration Office** (off Map p134; ☎ 0 2141 9889; Bldg B, Government Center, Soi 7, Th Chaeng Wattana; 🕒 8.30am-noon & 1-4.30pm Mon-Fri; 🚇 Mo Chit & access by taxi); see the Ministry of Foreign Affairs website (www.mfa.go.th) for more information.

Neighbouring countries also maintain embassies in Bangkok from which you can apply for a visa, but allow plenty of time.

GETTING AROUND

It can be tricky to decipher and pronounce Thailand's addresses. *Tà·nŏn* is a street, a *soi* is a laneway that runs off a *tà·nŏn* and a *đròrk* is an alley. In this book, 'Soi 6, Th Sukhumvit' means that Soi 6 runs off Th Sukhumvit. Building numbers often have confusing slashes and dashes, like 325/7-8 Th Charoen Krung. This stems from an old system of allocating property; the prefix in the address will be a help-ful locator once you arrive on the street, but don't count on it as an indicator of the building's proxim-ity to an intersection.

BUS

The city's public bus system, which is operated by the Bangkok Mass Transit Authority (BMTA), is the best option for reaching Banglamphu, Thewet, Dusit and other areas not serviced by the BTS or MRT. The buses are also sig-nificantly cheaper than the newer public-transport options, but are also subject to the hassles of traf-fic. Air-con bus fares range from 11B to 36B, while fan-cooled buses run from 6.50B to 8B. Smaller 'baht buses' ply major *soi* and cost 5B. For reviews in this guide, bus-transport details are preceded by the 🚌 symbol.

The BMTA operates a helpful website (www.bmta.co.th), and the *Bangkok Bus Guide* by thinknet, available at Kinokuniya Books (p83), is the most up-to-date route map available.

Hold on to your ticket as proof of purchase (an occasional formality).

BTS

The BTS or Skytrain (www. bts.co.th), represented by the 🚊 symbol in this guide, has revolutionised travel around the newer districts of Bangkok. Trains arrive every few minutes from 6am to midnight. Tickets will cost you from 15B to 40B. A one-day tourist pass (120B) is good for unlimited trips within a 24-hour period.

Most ticket machines at each station accept 5B and 10B coins only, but change is available from the staffed information booths. You can also buy value-stored tickets and pick up brochures detailing the various commuter and tourist passes at the info booths.

Once through the ticket gates, follow the signs for the desired line and terminus; you can transfer between the two lines at the Siam interchange station. The Sukhumvit line terminates in the north of the city at the Mo Chit station, next to Chatuchak Park, and follows Th Phayathai south to the interchange with the airport express at Phaya Thai and Siam interchange station at Th Rama I, before swinging east along Th Ploenchit and Th Sukhumvit to terminate at the On Nut station, near Soi 81. By the time you read this, the 5km extension southeast to Soi 107, Th Sukhumvit, should be finished.

The Silom line runs from the National Stadium station, near Siam Square, and soon after makes an abrupt turn to the southwest, continuing above Th Ratchadamri, down Th Silom to Th Narathiwat Ratchanakharin, then out Th Sathon, crossing the Mae Nam Chao Phraya and terminating at Wongwian Yai, in Thonburi.

MRT

The first line of Bangkok's subway, also known as the Metro (www. mrta.co.th), opened in 2004. It connects the railway station of Bang Sue with the following interchange stations connecting to the BTS stops: Chatuchak Park (Mo Chit BTS station), Sukhumvit (Asok BTS station) and Si Lom (Sala Daeng BTS station), and terminating at Hua Lamphong station. Trains operate from 5am to midnight and cost 16B to 41B.

For short-term visitors, the subway makes Hualamphong station and the convention centre easier to reach from Th Silom and Th Sukhumvit.

In reviews, MRT-transport details are preceded by the 🚇 symbol.

BOAT

For sights in Banglamphu, Ko Ratanakosin and some parts of Silom, the **Chao Phraya Express Boat** (☎ 0 2623 6001; www.chaophrayaexpress boat.com.th) is the most convenient option. The service runs from 6am to 7pm; you can buy tickets (13B to 32B) on board. Boats with yellow or red-and-orange flags are express boats. These boats run during peak times and therefore don't make every stop. A **tourist boat** (tickets 20B; ☇ 9.30am-3.30pm) runs from Tha Sathon (Map p93, B4) with stops at 10 major sightseeing piers. Hold on to your ticket as proof of purchase (an occasional formality).

Longtail *khlong* (canal) taxis zip around Bangkok's Khlong Saen Saeb, conducting quick trips from Tha Withayu (Map p79, E1), Tha Pratunam (Map p79, D1) and Tha Ratchathewi (Map p79, A1) to Tha Phan Fah (near Wat Saket; Map p51, E3). Fares cost from 9B to 21B and water taxis run from 6.15am to 7.30pm.

River-crossing ferries at the various piers cost 3.50B.

Private longtail boats can be hired for sightseeing trips at Tha Phra Athit, Tha Chang, Tha Oriental and Tha Tien.

In reviews, ferry-transport details are preceded by the ☇ symbol.

TAXI

Taxis in Bangkok are plentiful but victims of traffic vagaries. Always take meter taxis and insist on using the meters. Don't take taxis that quote a price (typically three times higher than the metered price). There's a 35B flag-fall charge, then it's 4.50B per kilometre for trips between 2km and 12km, 5B per kilometre between 13km and 20km and 5.50B per kilometre for more than 20km; in a traffic jam you pay 1.25B a minute. You pay a 50B surcharge for trips leaving the airport and all tolls.

TÚK-TÚK

These putt-putting three-wheeled vehicles are irresistible tourist-traps – they'll zip you to an over-priced tailor or jeweller regardless of your stated destination. For kicks, take them for short hops (within a neighbourhood); 50B is usually a fair price. Refuse to enter any unrequested shop, and skip the 10B sightseeing offers.

MOTORCYCLE TAXI

Need to be somewhere in a hurry in the middle of rush hour? A jaunt on a motorcycle taxi is guaranteed to be superquick and (hopefully) death-defying. Rides from the main road to the end of a *soi* are usually 10B. Women wearing skirts should remember to ride side-saddle.

CAR & MOTORCYCLE

You're either extremely patient or mad to drive in Bangkok. Even once you get somewhere, parking is usually a nightmare. You are required to have an International Driving Permit to drive in Bangkok. You'll pay around 30B/L for petrol.

Appearances may be deceiving, but there are road rules in Bangkok.

Car hire starts at around 1800B per day, but the rate is often cheaper if you hire by the week or month. Rental companies include **Avis** (Map p79, E2; ☎ 0 2251 1131; www. avisthailand.com; 2/12 Th Witthayu; ☼ 8am-6pm) and other international franchises.

If your car breaks down, you could try getting in touch with **CarWorld Club** (☎ 0 2612 9999; www. cwc.co.th), which offers roadside assistance.

PRACTICALITIES

BUSINESS HOURS

Bangkok is an on-the-go, seven-day-a-week town. Restaurants generally open from about 10am to 10pm, shops from 10am to 8pm. Businesses along Th Charoen Krung close on Sunday and street vendors don't sell on Monday. Most government offices are open from 8.30am to 4.30pm weekdays; some close from noon to 1pm for lunch, while others have Saturday hours (9am to 3pm). Banking hours are typically 8.30am to 3.30pm Monday to Friday.

ELECTRICITY

Electric currents in Thailand are 220V, 50 cycles. Most electrical wall outlets take the round, two-prong terminals, but some will take flat, two-bladed terminals and others will take both. Converters can be bought from electrical stores throughout the city.

HOLIDAYS

Lunar holidays change each year; for detailed information, check out www.tatnews.org.

New Year's Day 1 January
Maha Bucha (lunar) January–March
Chakri Day 6 April
Songkran Festival (lunar) April
Coronation Day 5 May
Visakha Bucha (lunar) May
Asaha Bucha (lunar) July
Khao Phansa (lunar) July
Queen's Birthday 12 August
Chulalongkorn Day 23 October
King's Birthday 5 December
Constitution Day 10 December

INTERNET

Internet access is widely available at internet cafes, costing anywhere from 20B to 150B per hour; wi-fi access at internet cafes is becoming more widespread. High-end hotels have wi-fi in the lobby and either wi-fi or

DIRECTORY

broadband in the rooms for an extra daily charge. Several cafes and restaurants around town offer free wi-fi.

LANGUAGE

Thailand's official language is Thai. The dialect from central Thailand has been adopted as the lingua franca, though regional dialects are still spoken. Thai is a tonal language, with five tones. Written Thai is read from left to right. Transliteration of Thai into the roman alphabet renders multiple (and sometimes contradictory) spellings. After every sentence, men affix the polite particle *kráp*, and women *kâ*.

BASICS

Greetings/Hello.	*sà·wàt·dee*
How are you?	*sà·bai dee mǎi*
I'm fine.	*sà·bai dee*
Excuse me.	*kǒr tôht*
Yes.	*châi*
No.	*mâi châi*
Thank you.	*kòrp kun*
You're welcome.	*mâi ʔen rai*
Do you speak English?	*pôot pah·sǎh ang·grìt dâi mǎi*
I (for male/female speaker)	*pǒm/dì·chǎn*
I don't understand.	*mâi kôw jai*
How much is this?	*née tôw rai*
That's too expensive.	*paang geun ʔai*

EATING & DRINKING

That was delicious!	*kòrp kun mâhk, a·ròy mâhk*
Please bring the bill.	*kǒr bin*
I'm allergic to…	*pǒm/dì·chǎn páa…*
I don't eat…	*pǒm/dì·chǎn gin… mâi dâi*
meat	*néu·a sàt*
chicken	*gài*
fish	*ʔlah*

Some common local dishes that you'll most likely come across:
gaang kěe·o wǎhn gài – green curry with chicken; usually not very spicy
gaang pèt gài/néu·a/mǒo – red curry with chicken/beef/pork; very spicy
góoay děeo lôok chín mǒo – noodle soup with pork balls
pàt tai – thin rice noodles fried with tofu, vegetables, egg and peanuts
đôm yam gûng – lemon-grass and prawn soup with mushrooms

EMERGENCIES

I'm sick.	*pǒm/dì·chǎn ʔòoay*
Help!	*chôoay dôoay*
Call a doctor!	*rêeak mǒr nòy*
Call the police!	*rêeak đam·ròoat nòy*

TIME & NUMBERS

today	*wan née*
tomorrow	*prûng née*
yesterday	*mêua wahn*

0	*sŏon*
1	*nèung*
2	*sŏrng*
3	*săhm*
4	*sèe*
5	*hâh*
6	*hòk*
7	*jèt*
8	*ƀàat*
9	*gôw*
10	*sìp*
11	*sìp-èt*
12	*sìp sŏrng*
13	*sìp săhm*
20	*yêe sìp*
21	*yêe sìp èt*
22	*yêe sìp sŏrng*
30	*săhm sìp*
100	*nèung róy*
200	*sŏrng róy*
1000	*nèung pan*

....

MONEY

CURRENCY

The basic unit of Thai currency is the baht (B), made up of 100 satang. Notes come in 20B, 50B, 100B, 500B and 1000B. Coins come in 1B, 2B, 5B, 10B and occasionally 25 or 50 satang. Go to 7-Eleven shops or hotels to break 1000B notes; don't expect a vendor or taxi to have change for 500B or anything larger.

ATMS

Automatic Teller Machines are widespread and usually accept Cirrus, Plus, Maestro, JCB and Visa cards.

CHANGING MONEY

Banks offer the best rates for changing money. They're generally open from 8.30am to 3.30pm Monday to Friday, but some have currency-exchange counters that operate from 8am to 8pm.

CREDIT CARDS

You'll have few problems using your credit card – especially if it's a Visa, MasterCard, Diners Club or Amex – at most higher-end hotels and restaurants. For 24-hour card cancellations or assistance:
American Express (☎ 0 2273 5544)
Diners Club (☎ 0 2238 3660)
MasterCard (☎ 001 800 11887 0663)
Visa (☎ 001 800 441 3485)

TRAVELLERS CHEQUES

Travellers cheques are easily cashed for a commission at major banks in Bangkok. Buy cheques in US dollars or British pounds to avoid possible hassles.

....

NEWSPAPERS & MAGAZINES

Bangkok has two English-language broadsheets: *Bangkok Post* and the *Nation*. Visit Asia Books (p120) and Kinokuniya Books (p83) for English-language material.

TELEPHONE

Most international roaming services work in Thailand, but a cheaper option is to buy a Thai SIM card. Thailand uses a GSM900/1800 system for its mobile providers. If you have an unlocked tri-band or quad-band GSM phone (most dual-band GSM phones will not work), you can buy a SIM card at just about any convenience store for as little as 100B. This can be topped up with prepaid or rechargeable cards, which start as low as 50B.

COUNTRY & CITY CODES

All Bangkok phone numbers have at least eight digits. Mobile phone numbers have an '8' prefix.

Thailand country code ☎ 66
Bangkok city code (land lines) ☎ 02

USEFUL PHONE NUMBERS

Local directory inquiries ☎ 1133
International operator ☎ 100
Reverse-charge (collect) ☎ 100

INTERNATIONAL DIRECT-DIAL CODES

Dial 001, 008 or 007 followed by:
Australia ☎ 61
Canada ☎ 1
Japan ☎ 81
New Zealand ☎ 64
South Africa ☎ 27
UK ☎ 44
USA ☎ 1

TIPPING

Tipping practices vary in Thailand, but many midrange and expensive restaurants add a 10% service charge to the bill in addition to a 7% VAT (value-added tax).

TOURIST INFORMATION

Beware of bogus tourist offices or officials purporting to be the real deal. The organisations below do not make travel arrangements.

Bangkok Information Center (Map p41, C1; ☎ 0 2225 7612-5; www.bangkoktourist.com; 17/1 Th Phra Athit; ⏱ 8am-7pm) Also has yellow information booths throughout the city.

Tourism Authority of Thailand Information Office (TAT; Map p51, E2; ☎ 0 2283 1500; cnr Th Ratchadamnoen Nok & Th Chakrapatdipong; ⏱ 8.30am-4.30pm)

Tourist Police (☎ 1155) For reporting crimes.

TRAVELLERS WITH DISABILITIES

Movement around the streets of Bangkok can be a complete nightmare for someone with impaired mobility – there are few sloping kerbs or wheelchair ramps, and many streets are best crossed via stair-heavy pedestrian crossings. Some travellers with disabilities hire a taxi or a private car and driver to see the sights, rather than taking tours, although it can be difficult to fit a wheelchair in the taxi boot. Five BTS stations have lifts: Asok, Chong Nonsi, Mo Chit, On Nut and Siam Square. You can travel for free from these stations if you show your disabled-association membership. Some hotel chains, such as Amari and Banyan Tree, are particularly aware of the needs of disabled travellers.

INFORMATION & ORGANISATIONS

Gimp on the Go (www.gimponthego.com)
Society for Accessible Travel & Hospitality (www.sath.org)

DIRECTORY

>INDEX

See also separate subindexes for See (p199), Do (p197), Shop (p200), Eat (p197), Drink (p197) and Play (p198).

000 map pages

INDEX

000 map pages